MAHABHARATA

The greatest epic of the world

Translated by :

Igen B.

With best wishes & lots of love,
ARJUNA

MANOJ PUBLICATIONS

Publishers

Manoj Publications
761, Main Road, Burari, Delhi-110084
Ph: 27611349, 27611116 Fax: 27611546,
Mobile: 9868112194
E-mail: manojpublications@vsnl.net
Website: www.manojpublications.com

Showroom:

Manoj Publications
1583-84, Dariba Kalan, Chandani Chowk, Delhi-6
Phone: 23262174, 23268216, Mobile: 9818753569

ISBN : 81-8133-471-X

Price : ●/-

Second Edition : 2005

Printers
Adarsh Printers
Naveen Shahdara, Delhi-110032

Mahabharata : *Igen B.*

CONTENTS

**Narayanam namaskritya naram chaiv narottamam!
Devim Saraswatim chaiv tato Jaymudiryet!!**

We pay obeisance to Lord Ganesh whose name spells the auspicious beginning of a task. We also bow our heads to Almighty Lord Narayana and to the Goddess of Learning, Saraswati to seek blessings for the success of this endeavour.

—Vyasa

KING SHANTANU MARRIES GANGA

The saga of Mahabharata begins with the mighty King Shantanu of Hastinapur. The ancestors of King Shantanu included illustrious names like King Bharata and his father King Dushyanta. King Dushyanta was invincible. His valour and courage was matchless. He had taken Shakuntala as his wife through a secret love marriage. She was the baby born out of the union of the great sage, Vishwamitra and Menaka, the beauty of the heaven. Sage Kanwa had brought up Shakuntala into youth. The secret love marrige of Dushyanta and Shakuntala resulted in the birth of Bharata. He was an incredible child who dared to force-open the Jaws of lions to count their teeth. Our country Bharat is infact named after him.

Once King Shantanu went to forest for hunting. The river Ganga flowed through that forest. The view along the river bank was very pleasing. He stopped his chariot at a spot and got down to take a walk. Suddenly, he saw a very beautiful young lady who had emerged from the depths and walked on the water as if she were walking on the ground. The King was amazed at her beauty and her feat of staying afloat. He fell in love with the strange beauty.

The beauty walked gracefully towards him and the King asked impatiently, "Who are you beautiful and why do you wander around in this wilderness?"

"Why do you wish to know?" the beauty chimed.

Her melodious voice made Shantanu's heart beat faster. He spoke in anxious voice, "O sweet lady! I have lost my heart to you. I am the King of Hastinapur and I wish earnestly to marry you."

"I can accept your proposal, O King. But there are two conditions to it."

"What conditions, Lady? Spell out. I will fulfil all your conditions."

"The first condition, is that you will never ask who I am or where I come from. The second, is that you will just watch whatever I shall do. You will not intervene. The day you violate any of these conditions I will leave you."

These conditions stunned King Shantanu. In normal situations such conditions would never have been acceptable to the King. But in the present case, Shantanu was too love stricken to refuse any demand of his lady love. So, he accepted both the conditions readily.

They became husband and wife by a secret love marriage.

As the King had met the lady on the bank of the river Ganga he started calling her 'Ganga' and brought her to his palace. The time flew away fast. King Shantanu spent all his time playing love games and romancing with Ganga neglecting his duties. His ministers looked after the affairs of the Kingdom. All the interests of Shantanu narrowed down to Ganga and her beauty.

❏ ❏

KILLING OF SEVEN SONS

In due course Queen Ganga gave birth to a son. The news of the birth of the son delighted King Shantanu. He gave away his precious necklace as reward to the maid who had brought the good news and rushed to Ganga's palace. But he was puzzled to see Ganga going towards the river with the newborn in her arms. He wanted to ask Ganga the reason but he remembered her condition and kept quiet. Shantanu followed Queen Ganga silently.

At the river bank, she turned back and smiled at King Shantanu. Then she put the newborn into the water and let the currents wash it away. It shocked King Shantanu. Queen Ganga returned with a smile of satisfaction on her face. Shantanu watched with unbelieving eyes and remained speechless.

A few weeks hence, Shantanu received the news of Ganga again being pregnant. He forgot about the sad fate of the earlier son and prayed for no repitition of the macabre act. He hoped to fondle his second son in his lap.

But his prayer was not answered and his hopes dashed. The news of the birth of his second son brought him to Ganga's palace where he found her again marching towards the river with the infant. He sadly staggered after her. Ganga again let the infant get carried away by the water currents.

Shantanu was grief stricken. His eyes shed tears of pain and anguish. But he could do or say nothing, being in the bind.

And thus, Queen Ganga murdered seven of her sons sired by King Shantanu.

The King watched and his heart bled. He could find no words to express his pain. Sometimes he would condemn himself, "What kind of a King you are? A woman kills your sons before your own eyes and you just play dumb witness! What's this cruel game? Fie on you!"

Shantanu was running out of patience. At last, he made up his mind to prevent the killing of his 8th son.

And sometime later, Queen Ganga gave birth to her 8th son and as usual, set out for the river to repeat her horror act. As she bent down to put the infant on the water currents, Shantanu thundered, "Now stop it! Enough is enough. Do you realise that you are murdering my 8th son? Do you want to put an end to my dynasty and deny the kindom a heir to the throne? Why, o why?"

Queen Ganga withdrew her hands that held the newborn. She straightened up and turned to say, "King! You have broken your promise by intervening. So, I must leave you. But before I depart I shall reveal to you the reason of my act. Dear King, I am Ganga of the heavens. Once, Sage Vashishta got very displeased with eight Vasu angels of heaven. He put a curse on them to take birth on earth as human beings and suffer the miseries of human life. The Vasu angels were terrified. Seven of them prayed to the sage for his pardon. The eight'th one remained defiant.

The sage pardoned the seven and said, *You will take birth on earth but shall die immediately after to return to the heavens. You won't live to suffer miseries. But this 8th unrepentant Vasu will live long to suffer all the pains and tragedies of the human life.* So, I transformed into a woman and married you simply to help the seven angels get freed of the curse. My job is done and I return to the heavens. But I shall take along your 8th son. I shall bring him up and fill him with incredible power of fortitude and forbearance to anable him to go through the harshest of the tragedies of the life. I'll return him to you as a youngman."

So saying, Ganga hugged her son to her bosom and flashed into the skies.

King Shantanu stood wonder strucked.

After Ganga's departure he returned to his palace deeply saddened.

❏ ❏

SHANTANU'S 8TH SON—DEVAVRATA

King Shantanu's life had become barren. He spent most of his time lost in the memories of Queen Ganga. Sometimes he broded over the tragedies of his seven sons and waited for the return of his 8th son.

He had lost interest in ruling the Kingdom.

At times, he became very restless. Then, he would go to the bank of the river Ganga and sit there for hours watching the waves with vacant eyes. He returned to his palace when he felt calmed down.

One day, when he arrived at the river bank, he found a teenager there who had a bow and arrows in his hand. The youngman evoked some feelings of belonging in Shantanu's heart and he went towards the teenager as if drawn by some force.

But before he could speak, his eyes widened to see a pleasant surprise.

Ganga was emerging out of the water.

Ganga came to him smiling and said, "King! This young man is your 8th son. I brought him up in a way that he is capable of handling any difficult situation or trouble. Guru Vashishta has imparted education on all subjects to him including martial training. I have named him 'Devavrata'. Go son," Ganga put her hand on the young man's head in blessing and spoke, "Now you go into the care of your father and I want you to make him happy."

And Ganga vanished.

King Shantanu's joy knew no bounds at getting his son back.

He brought his son to the palace and ordered his ministers to arrange for a grand celebration to welcome the arrival of the prince.

The very next day he called a meeting of his court and Devavrata was declared as the Crown Prince. Devavrata was very courageous and valiant. He was a dare devil too.

Once he was riding his horse along the borders of the Kingdom. He saw a neighbouring King marching in with a large army to invade Hastinapur. Devavrata challenged the invader and single handedly defeated the enemy army.

He took the King prisoner and produced him before his father in the court.

King Shantanu's chest swelled with pride at having such a brave son. But the loss of Ganga often made him a sad person.

Her memories lingered on in his mind.

❏ ❏

A STRANGE INCIDENT

The time was passing by at its merry speed. In Hastinapur, things had returned to normal and reasonable happy state. But one day an incident occured which changed the history of Kuru dynasty.

This incident too happened on the bank of river Ganga.

That day, as usual King Shantanu was taking a walk along the bank of Ganga when he sighted an extremely beautiful young lady. Shantanu again fell for this beauty just like he had done in the case of Ganga. He became love sick.

The young woman, Satyawati was the daughter of the chief of local fishermen. The King expressed his wish to marry the woman to her

father. The chief was a clever and a farsighted man. He put a condition before the King that the son of his daughter, Satyawati would be the Crown Prince and the heir to the throne.

The King at once rejected the condition. It was unthinkable for him to take away the right of his dear son Devavrata. And Shantanu had lost his seven sons as he had bound himself to the blind conditions of Ganga. He did not want to repeat the mistake again. So, he returned to the palace dejected and sad.

King Shantanu again became gloomy. Devavrata found out the reason of his father's sadness. He at once went to the chief of the fisherman in his chariot and said to him, "Please agree to the wish of my father. I promise to give up my right over the throne."

The father of Satyawati spoke, "But your sons can lay claim to the crown and create trouble for the sons of my daughter."

"I will stay bachelor all my life," Devavrata took a vow.

What else could Satyawati's father demand?

Devavrata set out for the palace with Satyawati in his chariot.

King Shantanu was greatly elated to see his heart throb, Satyawati coming to the palace in the chariot of Devavrata. He had been informed by the spies that the Crown Prince had gone to the fishermen village to bring Satyawati with due respect for his father after learning the cause of the father's sadness.

Satyawati's entry into the palace made Shantanu pride at his luck. He embraced his son and blessed him numerous times. Then, he led Satyawati to his palace.

The King was very anxious to know how Satyawati's father had so easily agreed to send her with Devavrata. So, at the very first chance he got, Shantanu questioned Satyawati about it. She told the King about the vows Devavrata had taken. The King was shocked to learn about the extremely severe vows his son had taken for him. He felt giddy and moaned, "So severe vows!"

And the King almost passed out in grief.

The news spread through the palaces. The severity of Devavrata's vows stunned everyone. The atmosphere became mournful. All the courtiers and the servants were upset. They had dreams of serving under Devavrata who had all the qualities of becoming a great king. It was disappointing.

Devavrata earned a new epithet 'Bhishma' which in Sankrit means 'extremely severe.' From that point of time, everyone called him Bhishma.

Queen Satyawati also sensed the tense air around for which she was responsible. She cursed herself for it.

Because of the unhappy situation, the King and the Queen could not fully enjoy the bliss which follows a marriage. A gloom always hung in the air.

The wheels of the time kept moving silently leaving history behind. Time is the greatest healer. The sadness created by Bhishma's vows also became a history. The King, Queen and the palace also regained natural air and ease.

In due course of time Queen Satyawati gave birth to two sons. One of them was named 'Chitrangada' and the other 'Vichitravirya.'

Then, King Shantanu died at ripe old age. After his death Chitrangada was crowned who lost his life in a battle shortly later. Vichitravirya succeeded him while he was still a minor.

When Vichitravirya became major, the Queen and Bhishma decided to get him married. And incidently the King of Kashi was organising the groom selections contest 'Swayamwara' for his three daughters. He had invited all the eligible kings and princes except the king of Hastinapur due to some old grudge.It was considered an insult to Hastinapur ruler. An angry Bhishma stormed into Kashi and siezed the three princesses. He forcibly brought all of them to Hastinapur for King Vichitravirya. The power and the valour of Bhishma was so daunting that no king or army could throw a challenge to him.

In Hastinapur, he ordered the preparations for the formal marriage ceremony to wed the princesses with King Vichitravirya.

The eldest princess of Kashi, Amba appealed to Queen Satyawati

MAHABHARATA—1

and Bhishma, "My heart has already accepted the prince of Shalva kingdom as husband. I request you to arrange to send me to him."

The Queen kindly accepted her request and asked Bhishma to send Amba to the prince of Shalva duly.

The other princesses, Ambika and Ambalika were married to the king Vichitravirya with great pomp and show.

The time passed by.

Seven years became history but Ambika and Ambalika could not bear any child.

Then Vichitravirya fell ill and passed away without siring any offspring.

As a result, there was no heir to the throne of Hastinapur. It created a great problem. A kingdom without any king or heir apparant is a bad omen.

Queen Satyawati was in a dilemma. No solution was in sight. She requested Bhishma to sit on the throne but he refused straight away as he was bound by his vow.

For Bhishma dishonouring his vow was ultimate shame which he could never accept.

❏ ❏

SAGE VYASA IN HASTINAPUR

After Bhishma's refusal to accept the crown, the queen Satyawati, in a desperate situation remembered her son, Vyasa, who she was blessed with by a boon of the sage, Parashar, before her marriage to King Shantanu. She summoned her sage son.

Sage Vyasa arrived to help his mother out.

Queen Satyawati wept at seeing her long forgotten son. Vyasa consoled her and asked, "Mother! why do you weep? Tell me, what is troubling you? If there is any solution to your problem I promise to work it out and I won't leave untill your trouble is over."

Vyasa's words calmed down Satyawati. She wiped off her tears and said, "Son! I know that you have great divine powers just like your father had. I regret to say that after the death of Vichitravirya, Kuru dynasty is coming to an end. There is no heir to the throne."

"Why is that, mother? Bhishma is there."

"He is in the bind of his vows. That is why I seek your help. I have full faith in you that you will end the dilemma your mother is in."

"Your faith in me is my order, mother. Just spell it out," Sage Vyasa said, "I have given you the word that I won't leave without solving your problem."

"So, listen son," Queen Satyawati spoke, "Ambika and Ambalika are widow queens of Vichitravirya who was your step brother. That relationship gives you the right to bless the widow queens to bear children to keep Kuru line going."

Vyasa bowed his head and went into a chamber.

Queen Satyawati sent Ambika into that chamber. As soon as she saw the ugly face of Sage Vyasa, she closed her eyes in horror. All through the blessing process she did not open her eyes. Later, Vyasa revealed to Queen Satyawati that Ambika shall give birth to a blind son. Otherwise the son will be healthy and powerful, he informed.

This saddened Satyawati. Then, she sent Ambalika to the chamber to get blessed. She was terrified to see Vyasa and turned pale. Sage Vyasa later disclosed that the son born to Ambalika will be of pale complexion and he will suffer from jaundice all his life. But he will be valiant nevertheless, the sage declared.

Queen Satyawati was not fully satisfied. She wanted a normal complete child with no handicaps. Hence, she ordered Ambika to go to Vyasa's chamber to get blassed again. She was too horrified to go to the sage again. So, she quietly dressed her maid in her royal finery and asked her to go to Vyasa in her place.

The maid had no inhibitions. She fearlessly marched into Vyasa's chamber and greeted the sage with enticing smile on her face. Her pleasant manners delighted Vyasa and he said after blessing her, "Your son will be wise, artful, diplomatic and a man of great learning. He will free you of the life of a maid servant."

Queen Satyawati was kept in dark about it.

In due course of time, the three women gave birth to one son each.

Ambika's blind son was named 'Dhritrashtra', Ambalika's son got the name 'Pandu' and the maid's son was christened 'Vidura'. Pandu was yellow coloured and Vidura was normal. All the three were brought up in royal style. When they grew up, Pandu sat on the throne because Dhritrashtra being blind was considered unfit to be the King. Vidura was appointed the Prime Minister.

Dhritrashtra was married to the princess Gandhari of Gandhar land. Gandhari was cultured and a pious woman. When she learnt that her husband was a born blind, she blind folded herself with a band and never took it off. Pandu married Pritha, the daughter of King Shoorsen. Pritha was better known as Kunti because of her beatiful hair. *Kuntal* is Sanskrit equivalent of 'Goldilocks.' Kunti was a simple and straight forward character. She had great respect for sages from the very young age. Once, Sage Durvasa came to visit King Shoorsen. Young Kunti looked after him with such care and devotion that the pleased sage blessed her with a divine mantra with which she could invoke any god. She was very young. Out of childish curiosity, Kunti invoked Sun god. Sun god appeared and blessed her with a child. She was unmarried and virgin. When the child was born, she put it in a basket and placed the basket on the river water to be carried away. A weaver found the basket and started rearing the child as his own.

Gandhari gave birth to hundred sons and a daughter. The daughter's name was Dushala. She was maried to the King of Sindhu, Jaidratha. The eldest of the Dhritrashtra-Gandhari sons was called Duryodhana.

Kunti became the mother of three sons, Yudhishthira, Bheema and Arjuna, in that order. Yudhishthira and Arjuna were boons of Lord Dharamaraja and Lord Indra. King Pandu had another queen too named Madri who was the princess of Madra kingdom. Two sons were born to Madri, namely, Nakula and Sahdeva. Thus, Pandu had five sons who later became famous as Pandavas and Dhritrashtra's hundred sons came to be known as Kauravas.

One day, King Pandu went on a hunting trip. There, by mistake his arrow hit a sage who was romancing with his wife. Upon hearing a human cry, Pandu ran to the place where lay the sage dying wounded by his arrow. The dying sage put a curse on Pandu, "When you will go near your wife driven by desire to make love, you shall die like I am dying." Later one day, Pandu blinded by the beauty of Madri went near her siezed by an irresistible wish to make love to her. The curse worked and King Pandu died instantly. Madri became Sati with the King. Thus, the responsibility of bringing up all the five sons of Pandu fell on Kunti.

After the death of King Pandu, his eldest son, Yudhishthira had the right to sit on the throne but he was merely a kid. Hence, Dhritrashtra was installed on the throne temporarily as the caretaker King to serve until Yudhishthira did not become a major.

Although Dhritrashtra was a temporary King yet he wanted to lay permanent claim to the throne for the sake of his ambitious son Duryodhana who wished to become the Crown Prince without delay. Behind this intrigue, Gandhari's brother, Shakuni's cunning mind was working overtime. He lost no opportunity to sow the seeds of distrust and enmity between Pandavas and Kauravas. Duryodhana had become bitter enemy of Pandava brothers. But he dared not come out openely against Pandavas because he feared Bheema. Bheema was the mightiest in physical power among all Pandavas and Kauravas.

Duryodhana often hatched schemes to kill Pandavas.

One day, Pandava and Kaurava princes were playing ball in the ground. Somehow the ball fell in a nearby well. The princes ran to it and peeped inside. The well was deep and down there the ball was floating over water. While leaning into the well, the ring of Yudhishthira slipped off his finger and fell into the well.

No prince dared to go down into the well to retrieve the ball and the ring. No one knew what to do. Just then, a Brahmin happened to pass by. He saw the princely kids crowding around the well. He asked them what was going on and why all the kids had sad faces.

The Brahmin had an impressive personality. He had a bow in his hand and arrowful quiver hung by his left shoulder.

Yudhishthira bowed to the Brahmin and told him their problem. The Brahmin assured them, "Don't worry kids. I will get your ball and the ring out of the well."

Tall grass grew around the ground. He asked the kids to get him some long stalks of the tall grass or beanpoles. He sharpened one end of the bean-poles. He shot a bean stalk like an arrow aimed at the ball. The stalk went into the ball. The pointed end of the next stalk pierced the open end of the first stalk. He shot many other stalks creating a long chain of stalks in this way which reached up the well. The Brahmin pulled out the stalk chain and retrieved the ball.

This delighted the princely kids.

Another mantra invoked arrow brought out the ring of the prince Yudhishtrira.

The princes were amazed to see the archery skill of the Brahmin. It was an impressive show. Infact, the Brahmin was none other than the great master of archery, Dronacharya. He was a well-known name among archers. Dronacharya was married to Kripi, the sister of Kripacharya. Kripacharya used to teach princes. Dronacharya had a son named Ashwatthama whom he loved dearly. Due to poverty he could not fulfil many of the wishes of his loved son. It always pained him. He could do little as no permanent employment was coming his way which worried him.

Once, he remembered the words of his classmate, prince Drupada. When both were studying together at the *ashram* of Sage Agnivesh, he used to say, "Friend Drona! Once I become King everything I own will be yours as well. I shall never let you rot in poverty. You must come to my court any time you wish."

One day, Dronacharya's son complained to him that his friends often made fun of him due to their poverty. It hurt the father deeply. So, he decided to go to his classfellow friend of one time to seek his help. Drupada had become the King. Hopefully, Dronacharya walked into the court of King Drupada accompanied by his wife and the son. He was in for a shock. The King refused to recognise his ex-classfellow. He even insulted Dronacharya and got him expelled from his court.

Dronacharya declared in angry voice, "Drupada! I will take revenge on you for this humiliation."

Thus, he had returned a sadder man.

Little did he realise that on that day luck was going to smile on him. The princes requested him to go along with them to meet their granduncle, Bhishma. Dronacharya accepted their suggestion and met the great warrior Bhishma. Bhishma was greatly impressed with the knowledge and the archery skills of Dronacharya. Without any hesitation he appointed Dronacharya as the Royal Teacher to teach the princes the art of warfare and weapon training.

Dronacharya was extremely happy to find a well paid permanent employment. He earnestly got down to the job of teaching the princes.

Almost all the princes were good learners. The first term of education ended soon. Guru Dronacharya decided to test his pupil's skills. He placed a wooden bird on a branch of a tree and asked his students to get ready with their bows and arrows.

The students got ready at a distance with arrows put to the strings of their bows in shooting position. Then, Guru told them about the target. It was the bird's eye.

Then, he asked every pupil, "What do you see?"

Being the eldest of all, Yudhishthira was supposed to be the first one to reply. He said, "The tree, branch and the bird."

"It's no good. Stand aside."

The others who followed him gave somewhat similar answers. Guru didn't look satisfied. When the turn of Arjuna came, he repeated the question, "What do you see?"

Arjuna's reply was brief, "Only the bird's eye."

Without waiting for Guru's next command, he shot his arrow.

The arrow hit the eye of the bird.

The others clapped hands. Guru Drona was very impressed. He praised Arjuna's concentration of mind on target and hugged him endearingly.

From that moment, Arjuna became his favourite pupil.

One day Guru Drona was sitting with his wards when a boy named Eklavya came to him and requested him to enrol him too as his student. Eklavya was a tribal boy. Drona looked at his princely students for reactions. The princes were not enthusiastic. Many of them had look of disapproval. Guru Drona realised that the princes didn't want to make a lowly tribal their classfellow. He was helpless. He could not keep Eklavya under his tutelage on his own because he was technically an employee of the royal family appointed by Bhishma to train the princes

24

only. It was not his private *ashram*. So, he had to refuse admission to that tribal boy.

But that tribal boy had come to him with an iron determination.

After Drona expressed his inability to admit him, he respectfully paid obeisance to Guru Drona and picked up a handful of soil from the ground underneath the feet of Drona. He put his hand to his forehead and departed.

He didn't go back to his home. He went to the nearby forest. There he collected a heap of clay and mixed in it the handful of soil he had brought. Then, he created a clay model of Guru Drona.

Now, everyday he would touch the feet of the clay model and practise archery on his own.

❑ ❑

EKLAVYA PAYS *GURUDAKSHINA*

One day, Eklavya was busy in practising arrow shooting when a dog appeared there and started barking at him.

He tried to drive away the dog but it wouldn't go. When it went on for sometime, Eklavya lost his temper and shot seven arrows at the dog. The arrows expertly stitched the mouth of the dog shut without seriously wounding it. The dog ran away yelping and reached where Drona lived as a royal teacher.

The dog incidently belonged to one of the princes.

The stitched mouth of the dog amazed the princes. Guru Drona himself was stunned to watch the archery skill of whoever had done it. Guru decided to follow the paw marks with the princes to see where the dog had met such fate.

They reached the place where Eklavya was busy in practice. Guru Drona at once recognised him. He was delighted.

He asked, "Did you do that to the dog?"

Eklavya bent down on his knees to pay obeisance to him and spoke, "Yes, the dog was disturbing my practice."

Guru Drona had a dream that his favourite pupil Arjuna would one day be the matchless archer of the world. Now he was doubtful about it. Eklavya had the talent to beat Arjuna.

So, he asked in surprise, "Who is your Guru?"

"You, sir. You are my Guru."

"I...?" Drona was stunned and he queried, "How come?"

"O Guru! Look here...," Eklavya pointed to the clay model of Drona and added, "On that day you did not accept me as your student. But I had accepted you as my Guru in my heart. Whatever skill I have gained today is the gift of your blessing."

"Then pupil! You must pay me *gurudakshina*."

When Eklavya asked what he wanted, Drona asked for the thumb of Eklavya. Eklavya, without second thought, cut off his thumb and presented it to Guru Drona.

In ancient India, it was a custom that a student gave to his guru whatever he asked in *gurudakshina* (Guru's fee) at the end of the education.

Thus, Drona cleared the way of his favourite student Arjuna of any challenge in becoming the greatest archer.

Eklavya set up an unique example of the devotion of guru.

❏ ❏

CONTESTS AMONG PRINCES

In due course, arms training of the princes came to an end. Guru Drona took all his students to Grandman Bhishma and announced the completion of their weapons education. To test the skills of the princes the Grandman proposed to hold a contest. Guru Drona gladly agreed to it as he had full faith in his students.

The days of the contests were fixed and a puplic declaration was made that to mark the end of the arms education of the princes, a contest was being organised which would be open to the public.

PRINCES SHOW THEIR SKILLS

The venue of the contests was Hastinapur's Royal games centre. It was a festive atmosphere there on that day. In a special block, King Dhritrashtra, Grandman Bhishma, Prime Minister Vidura, other ministers and chieftans were seated. In another block, sat high officials, the rich and famous and the prominent citizins. All around the games ground there were staired seating systems for the public.

The King gave the signal and the show began.

Guru Drona brought Arjuna first and asked him to demonstrate his power. He showed his archery skills. First, simple shooting power and then, fierce weapon power. Arjuna shot an arrow into the ground which created leaping flames. The people got scared. But he shot another arrow skywards and it brought down heavy showers. It drew an thundering applause from the public. The people hailed Arjuna. All had to agree that he was the deadliest archer in business.

The next demonstration was by mace wielders.

There were two mightiest mace wielders, Bheema and Duryodhana. They had natural dislike for each other and carried several grudges against each other. Duryodhana lived in fear of Bheema.

He had secretly plotted to kill Bheema many times. Once he had given poisoned food to Bheema. And unconscious Bheema was thrown into a river. He sank down to reach the serpent world where he met a man-o-snake who turned out to be Bheema's maternal side grand father by some old relationship. The old man was so pleased to meet his overland grand child that he blassed Bheema with the physical power of one thousand elephants through his divine powers.

Thus, Bheema had returned mightier than before.

But he did not know the treachery of Duryodhana. Whenever they clashed Bheema always gained upper hand.

Guru Drona signalled for the fight to begin. The mace battle between Bheema and Duryodhana started.

Suddenly Guru realised that the two were fighting real battle and were going for the kill. Ashwatthama also noted it and he jumped between the battlers and stopped the fight with great difficulty.

KARNA'S CHALLENGE TO ARJUNA

As the contests were coming to end, Karna stormed into the venue. The same child whom Kunti had abandoned to river currents had grown into mighty Karna, the weaver's fondling child. He had become a bosom friend of Duryodhana and himself was an archer of great skill. The praise Arjuna had earned for his archery had annoyed Karna. He threw a challenge, "Guru Dronacharya! You have praised Arjuna sky high and described him as matchless. I also want to show my archery skills for comparison."

"Why not, Karna? You are welcome," Guru Drona said and invited, "You can show us your skills."

"But I don't play games," Karna said testily and announced, "I want a real battle with Arjuna."

The royal priest Kripacharya considered Karna's unjustified demand an unsporting gesture. So, he objected, "This contest is for the princes. And not for the children of weavers. It is not permissible."

Duryodhana rose up from his seat and supported his friend Karna, "Who says that Karna is no prince? I declare Karna the King of Anga land with immediate effect."

Then, Arjuna went to the priest Kripacharya and with his permission spoke to Karna, "Listen Karna! This world is full of warriors. There are great many. No one considers himself invincible. So do I. But by challenging me for a real battle you have spoiled the spirit of this sporting event. You showed arrogance instead of your archery skills. I will break your arrogant pride one day, I promise."

The people supported Arjuna and Karna felt belittled.

Grandman Bhishma announced the closure of the event.

Duryodhana didn't like Grandman's decision. He wanted battle between Karna and Arjuna right then and there. But who could openly disagree with Grandman Bhishma?

❑ ❑

DRONA'S GURUDAKSHINA DRUPADA AS PRISONER

Guru Dronacharya was now living a life of happiness and great honour. The days of poverty were over. He had become prosperous. Only thing that still rankled him was his inability to take revenge on King Drupada for his insulting behaviour to him. The humiliation he suffered was not easy to forget. He always brooded over it.

Suddenly, one day he got an idea.

The next day, he summoned all his princely students to him and announced. "Dear pupil! I have imparted you the knowledge of warfare, the use of various weapons and all the martial techniques. Now, as per tradition I want you to pay me *gurudakshina.*"

The princes asked him what he wished of them.

Guru Drona spelled out his demand. "Before I came to Hastinapur I had gone to the court of King Drupada. He had been my classfellow and a close friend when we were students. But he refused to recognise me and expelled me after subjecting me to great humiliation. As a revenge act, I want him brought to me as a prisoner. That's all I ask of you."

Pandavas took a vow to fulfil the task.

But Kauravas backed out since they hated to join any venture that Pandavas undertook.

The very next day, Pandavas brought King Drupada as prisoner on their own might and produced him before Guru Drona. It pleased him. Drupada stood before Drona in shame and dishonour.

Thus Pandaves paid *gurudakshina* to their teacher.

Draupadi, the daughter of King Drupada later married Pandavas.

❏ ❏

DURYODHANA'S TRICK
PANDAVAS IN LAC-HOUSE

Pandavas were one better than Kauravas in every field. The Kauravas were arrogant but Pandavas were kind and polite. The people of Hastinapur favoured Pandavas, spies reported. They wanted Pandu's eldest son, Yudhishthira declared as Crown Prince sooner the better. All wished to see Dhritrashtra duly hand over the throne to him. So, one day, Grandman Bhishma called the meeting of the court and got a proposal to that effect accepted. Dhritrashtra was forced to prepare to declare Yudhishthira as the Crown Prince although he wanted his son, Duryodhana to wear that crown.

Yudhishthira besides being the eldest prince, was a model of patience, truthfulness, kindness, fairness and goodwill for others.

Duryodhana could not tolerate it. His right of becoming Crown Prince being taken away upset him. Out of anger and jealousy he began thinking of ways of physically destroying Pandavas to clear his path to the throne. A fair was being held in Varnavat during those days. Duryodhana hatched a horrible plot with the help of a minister named Purochana. They got a house made of lac constructed overnight at Varnavat. Then, Duryodhana approached his father, King Dhritrashtra and suggested, "Father! I request you to send my Pandava brothers along with mother Kunti to Varnavat fair. They will like it."

Dhritrashtra was surprised to hear his son say something nice for Pandavas. He suspected nothing. So, he sent Yudhishthira to the fair in the capacity of the Crown Prince.

When the lac house was planned the engineers and the workers were bought through bribes by Duryodhana and his henchmen. So they kept quite except one engineer who suspected the intentions of Duryodhana.

He quietly informed Prime Minister Vidura about the proposed lac house. Vidura told the engineer about his counter plan and asked him to act on it.

When Pandavas were departing from Hastinapur Vidura informed them of the suspected plot. He also revealed to them the escape plan. Yudhishthira took leave of the King and set out for Varnavat along with his brothers and the mother.

At Varnavat, the agents of Duryodhana put up Yudhishthra and party in the same lac-house. Lac is a highly inflammable substance.

Vidura's confident engineer had constructed a secret escape tunnel out of the lac-house with the help of some faithful workers. Vidura had told Yudhishthira about that tunnel.

The evil Duryodhana had made all arrangements to see that Pandavas did not come out alive.

The fair was going on.

Pandavas roamed around the fair during the day and in the evening they returned to lac-house. They would close all doors and then would descend into the safe tunnel to sleep the night. They kept close watch on the activities of Purochana.

The last day of the fair arrived.

Yudhishthira organised a yajna at the end of which Brahmins and the priests were seen off with appropriate alms and gifts.

It was announced that after the night's stay at lac-house, Pandavas would depart in the morning for home.

It was a moonless dark night. Pandavas and Kunti went to the usual safe place to sleep. So far nothing had happened. So, they were sure that something ugly would happen that night if something was to happen. They were alert and ready fully armed.

Suddenly, shortly past midnight, the lac-house was on fire.

The flames leapt high. Lac-house became an inferno.

But Pandavas were safe. As soon as fire was noticed they had escaped through the tunnel and reached the river bank where a boat waited for them with an oarsman as preplanned by wise Vidura. They boarded the boat and safely landed on the other side of the river.

❏ ❏

GRIEF STRICKEN
DHRITRASHTRA AND DURYODHANA

As soon as the news of the burning of the lac-house and the perishment of Pandavas and their mother reached Hastinapur, the kingdom was hit by shock waves.

Duryodhana was very pleased inwardly but outwardly he put on an act of being in grief and ran towards Varnavat wailing.

There, he found burnt out bodies of the minister, Purochana, a guard, a servent, a woman and five men.

The death of his agent Purochana surprised Duryodhana. It was he who was to set fire to the house. Why didn't he save himself, Duryodhana wondered.

The fact was that it was Bheema who had set the fire. He wanted to kill all the accomplices of Duryodhana present in the house to weaken the enemy's strength. The burnt woman was not Kunti. She

was a homeless woman who had sought refuge along with her five sons in that house by some coincidence.

Duryodhana returned after his survey.

He declared a state of mourning in the kingdom at once. Outwardly, Dhritrashtra and Duryodhana were showing grief stricken faces but in their hearts they were feeling happy.

They thought that now, Duryodhana's way was clear. All the hurdles of his way to the throne had been taken care of. Grandman Bhishma and other courtiers were in a state of shock and their sadness was beyond words. Their minds were too benumbed to suspect any foul play.

❑ ❑

PANDAVAS IN THE WILDS

On the other side of the river Ganga, Pandavas and Kunti entered into the forest. After a great trouble and hardships they reached the dense growths. They flopped down deadly tired under a bunyan tree. All of them were hungry and thirsty. Their bodies were exhausted. Kunti was in a very bad condition. All fell asleep except Bheema.

Bheema was pained that his mother and the four brothers were hungry. He set out to look for some water. He found a clear water pond just a little distance away. The water was refreshingly cold. He drank the water to his hearts content. Then, he made a cup of lotus petals and came back with water in it.

First, he thought of waking up Kunti and the brothers to offer water. Then, he felt that he shouldn't disturb their sleep. The water had energized him. So, he stood gurading his sleeping mother and brothers.

BHEEMA KILLS HIDIMB MARRIES HIDIMBA

The forest where Pandavas lay sleeping fell into the zone of a demon, named Hidimb. He was cruel, horrible and a maneater. Hidimb lived on a tree with his sister, Hidimba. Hidimb would often set out in the evening on hunt and would sleep on the tree after satisfying his hunger. On that day, he was resting on the tree after making meals of two wild bulls. The human smell made him again feel hungry. He spoke to his sister, "I get smell of humans from the north direction. Go and see. Tell me about it. Long time not eaten human flesh."

Hidimba got down and went towards north. She too was feeling hungry for human flesh. She came to the spot where Pandavas were asleep. And there was a woman too. She was very pleased. Then, she saw Bheema who was sitting on a rock keeping a watch. Hidimba at once fell for the muscular body of Bheema. She forgot about the hunger for human flesh and the mission her brother had sent her on. She just wished to be the woman of that strong built young man. She transformed herself into a beauteous human lady and walked musically towards Bheema. On finding a stunning beauty loaded with finery approaching him, Bheema stood up.

Before he could find words, Hidimaba spoke, "O Dear! Who are you? What a body! Marvellous! Are these sleeping people with you? Never mind. I have fallen in love with you at first sight. You must marry me, please. This area belongs to my demon brother Hidimb. He is very cruel and is a man-eater. He plans to eat you all. So I request you to get your people to some safe place. I will help you deal with my brother with my sorcery powers."

Bheema said in reaction, "O Beauty! Don't worry about my family. I don't want to disturb the sleep of my mother and brothers. If your brother comes here to make trouble I will teach him a lesson."

Infact, the demon Hidimb had followed his sister out of impatience. When he saw his sister in the human guise talking romantically to a young man, the demon lost his temper, "You bad lowly character! I will teach you a lesson. By falling for a human you have shamed the demon race. You are a big disgrace. I will kill your human lover."

Hidimb lunged at his sister very aggressively and tried to grab her hand but Bheema intervened. He blocked the hand of Hidimb and caught his wrist in his grip. Bheema roared, "How dare you use force against a woman, evil creature! Face me if you have guts! You coward!"

The mighty demon flew in a rage at being handled and challenged by a mere human being. He freed his hand from Bheema's grip and landed a blow on the back of Bheema's neck.

The blow was mighty but Bheema stood his ground bravely. He

counter attacked and a battle of titans began. The booming sounds of blows woke up Kunti and the four sleeping Pandavas. The wild creatures too were scared and they ran helter and skelter.

When the brothers saw Bheema battling a mighty demon single handedly, they came forward to help. But they stopped in their tracks when Bheema picked up Hidimb over his head like a toy and threw him down on the ground with great force.

Hidimb groaned in pain and after a few hiccupps died.

Then, Arjuna said to Yudhishthira, "Brother! We must leave this place at once. Because the mighty demon's death is a big news and spies of Duryodhana will trace us as they know that only brother Bheema can do it."

All the Pandavas agreed to it and walked ahead after drinking water. Hidimba followed them quietly.

After travelling for quite some distance, Kunti happened to look back. She was surprised to find a beautiful woman following them. Kunti asked, "Who are you and why do you follow us?"

Hidimba moved forward and touched the feet of Kunti and revealed, "Mother! I am Hidimba. The demon your son killed a while ago was my brother. So, I am too from demonic family," then she added shyly, "I'm impressed by the bravery of your son. I have accepted him as my husband by heart. Now whatever you order."

Kunti looked towards Bheema who remained speechless and flushed. She knew that her son too was interested in the union. Kunti said, "Alright daughter! If you two accept each other. Then it is God's will. Why should I object to it? You can take my son. But do give him to us back every evening when it becomes dark because in this dark forest we need his mighty protection."

Hidimba departed with Bheema in the morning. Kunti and the rest of Pandavas found out a safe shelter to live. Thus, Bheema would go to Hidimba in the mornings and would come back to his mother and the brothers to stay for the nights.

❑ ❑

Many months went by as Pandavas continued their stay in that forest. Meanwhile, Hidimba gave birth to a son who was christened 'Gatotakacha'. He was as mighty as his father Bheema. As Gototakacha was son of a demoness mother, he looked like a grown up young man ever as a kid.

One day, Pandavas and Kunti decided to go to some other place because staying at a particular place was dangerous. Kunti asked Gatotakacha to stay back for the protection of his mother and to look after her. The boy spoke to Bheema, "Father! I will stay back with my mother according to grandma's order. But I request you not to forget us. Whenever you need me just give a call. You will find me by your side."

The Pandavas and Kunti blessed Gatotakacha and moved on.

❏ ❏

PANDAVAS MEET SAGE VYASA

Even after a journey of several days, Pandavas did not come across any safe and suitable place to stay for some time. They wandered around.

One day, they suddenly ran into Sage Vyasa. Pandava brothers did not know him but they paid their respects to the sage. Kunti knew him. When after the death of King Pandu, the Queen mother Satyawati had expressed her wish to renounce royal life to live like an ascetic in Sage Vyasa's *ashram* then Vyasa had himself come to escort Satyawati.

Kunti burst into tears as soon as she recognised him and she narrated the entire story to him.

Sage Vyasa was omniscent. He consoled Kunti, "Daughter! the time changes. Good days and bad days keep coming and going. Sadness has seeds of happiness in it. A man should stay on the path of truth and wait for the good tidings patiently."

Sage Vyasa directed them towards a nearby town.

The town was called 'Ekchakra'. Pandavas started living there in a Brahmin's house in disgaise. The brothers would set out to seek alms during the day and at night they would rest at that house. The people took them for Brahmins because they lived like Brahmins do.

Pandavas would hand over to Kunti whatever food they collected in alms. Kunti would divide the entire food in two portions, one for mighty Bheema and the other would suffice for the rest five.

One day, Kunti fell ill. Yudhishthira asked Bheema to stay home to look after her. The rest of the brothers went away.

Suddenly Kunti heard sounds of wailing and weeping coming from the rooms Brahmin family occupied.

Kunti said, "Son! …The Brahmin family appears to be in some trouble. Let me find out about it."

And she went to their rooms. She came back after a while and informed, "The family is in big trouble. Poor people."

By then, the Pandava brothers had also returned. Yudhishthira asked, "What trouble are you talking about, mother?"

Kunti said, "Sons! A horrible demon named 'Bakasura' is said to live on a nearby hill. He used to come to this town to go on rampage. Then people requested to the demon not to go on the destruction and killing spree. In return they agreed to send to the demon two buffaloes, a human and the other food stuff everyday. Today it is the turn of the son of the Brahmin. That was why the family was weeping. I asked them to stop mourning and promised them that my son Bheema would free the town from the terror of that demon."

Yudhishthira, Arjunas, Nakula and Sahdeva looked at Bheema.

He spoke, "I will honour your word, mother. The family has given us shelter. We are duty bound to help them out."

All the brothers nodded their heads in approval and expressed good wishes to Bheema.

❑ ❑

BHEEMA BLASTS BAKASURA

The next day, Bheema drove to the demon's hill with a cartload of food stuffs. There, he unharnessed the buffaloes from the cart and set them free to run into the jungle. Then, he sat down to eat the food meant for Bakasura. He feasted joyfully. The horrible Bakasura came out of his cave and found Bheema gobbling his food. It angered him and he thundered, "What stupid human is this who eats my food before my own eyes? Gone mad with death wish?"

Bheema ignored Bakasura and kept merrily eating food smacking his lips. The demon rushed towards Bheema madly screaming in anger. He gave Bheema a double fisted whack on his back. It made no impression on Bheema who kept sitting and licking his fingers. Bakasura's blood boiled. He ran to a tree to uproot it for rushing Bheema.

Bheema was finishing the feast. He drank water and burped with great satisfaction. Then, he rose up.

Bakasura had come back with an uprooted tree. He tried to hit Bheema with it but Bheema blocked it with one hand. A surprised Bakasura wondered, "Huh! Can a human be so powerful?"

He got no time to solve the puzzle. Bheema's fist had exploded on him. The blow threw Bakasura back to crash against the tree. The tree and Bakasura both fell down. Bheema gave him no chance to gather himself. Bheema's foot planted on chest pinned down the demon. Then, he caught the demon's leg and pulled it headwards. There were a series of terrible cracking sounds. First, the ribs of the demon snapped and then, the spine broke with exploding sound which made the nearby rocks slide down.

The painful cries of dying Bakasura echoed from the hills.

Bheema lassoed the neck of Bakasura with a piece of cloth and dragged his body down hill. In town, he placed Bakasura's body on a cross road and slipped away.

When some one saw the demon's body the news of Bakasura's death spread around. The people collected there in no time. Soon everyone appeared to be running into the same direction. The liberation from the demon's terror elated one and all.

Soon the question arose, "Who killed Bakasura and then dragged his body into the town?"

It was a puzzle.

The Brahmin in whose house Pandavas lived was also in the crowd. He had strict instructions no to reveal the truth about the killing of Bakasura. Kunti and Pandavas had insisted on it.

The Brahmin himself was greatly surprised as others were puzzled. The people knew that the Brahmin had to send his son to Bakasura on that day. So, they suspected that the Brahmin must know something about the death of the demon. The people surrounded the Brahmin and started asking questions. He tried to deflect the questions. But people wanted the truth. They forced him to reveal the truth.

He had to tell, "All right, if you want to know I shall tell. When my family was weeping for our son a Brahmin appeared at my door. I invited him in. He asked why members of my family were weeping. I tried to put him off but he insisted on knowing the reason. I told him about the demon Bakasura. The Brahmin asked us not to worry. He said that he would go to Bakasura with his food in place of my son. He claimed that he knew some mantra or sorcery which could kill the demon. We protested but he won't listen. I had to agree and let him go with food and buffaloes. I think it is the doing of that Brahmin."

The people were satisfied and went to their homes in happy mood.

❑ ❑

YAJNA FOR CHILD BY PANCHALA KING

Since Pandavas had taken Panchala King, Drupada to Dronacharya as prisoner, he had been suffering in a burning desire to take revenge on Drona. He was childless. He wanted a son who could give it back to Drona. As he was getting old he sought the help of sages performed 'Putreshti Yajna' to get blessed with a son.

At the end of the Yajna, a divine man emerged from the Yajna flames. His face glowed and he wore shining arms. He looked every bit a great warrior.

A voice announced, "Drupada! This person is your son. Name him 'Dhrishtadhyumana'. He will fulfil all the wishes a father can have of his son."

King Drupada was elated. His ministers and courtiers were happy.

Just then, a bewitching beauty of darkish complexion rose from the flames. Her facial features were sharply chiselled. She had almond shaped dreamy eyes and her hair was shimmering. She was stunning.

The divine voice spoke again, "She is your daughter, Drupada. Name her 'Krishnaa'.

King Drupada was ecstatic. It was too good and too true as well.

The pride of King Drupada soared.

This daughter of Drupada became famous as Draupadi, the true heroine of Mahabharata.

❑ ❑

PANDAVAS MOVE TO PANCHALA

Pandavas had lived in Ekchakra town for quite some time.

They must move. Since Bheema killed Bakasura there was always a danger of Duryodhana's agents tracing them out. Kunti said to her sons one day, "We must leave this place. As soon as the news of killing of Bakasura reaches Duryodhana he would send his agents to investigate at once. He knows that no ordinary mortal can kill Bakasura. He will do anything. This town may suffer because of us."

Pandava brothers agreed and moved towards Panchala.

After crossing a dense forest they reached the bank of river Ganga. Arjuna was leading them with a fire torch in his hand.

Suddenly, he saw the dim figure of a chariot racing at them. The chariot stopped near Arjuna and a harsh voice warned, "Stop or you will get killed. Don't you now that it is time for the bath of the divine races like Yakshas, Gandharvas and the others. Go back!"

Pandavas were surprised. But they could not make out who was threatening them.

Arjuna patiently heard the challenge and asked, "O Divine Person! Who are you? Don't you know that Ganga is a sacred river open to all and at all times. It is no one's private property. So, who are you to stop us?"

The divine figure said angrily, "Lowly human! I am the Gandharva King, Angarparva. My power and valour is well-known all over. The bank area on the both sides of this river is my domain. Even gods and angels can't tread this area without my permission. You are a mere human. This is my last warning, go back or perish for your foollishness."

The arrogant boast of the speaker annoyed Arjuna.

He spoke in harsh voice, "Divine man! You should not be so impolite if you are really divine. Don't take the other one for a weakling without knowing his power. This world in not bereft of warriors. May be, you scare those who are weaklings. For your arragance I am forced to challenge you even at this ungodly hour."

Arjuna's rebuke angered Angarparva to no extent. He drew out his sword rushed towards Arjuna challenging.

Arjuna blocked Angarparva's sword on his torch and thundered, "Arrogant Gandharva! Save yourself. It appears that you have never faced a true warrior or your language would not have been so crude and lowly."

He threw his fire torch at Angarparva after invoking it with a mantra. The torch torched the chariot of Angarparva who jumped down. Arjuna cought him by hair and dragged him into the presence of Kunti and Yudhishthira. The wives of Angarparva had seen their husband disgraced. They raced to Yudhishthira and begged for mercy for their husband.

Yudhishthira took pity on them and spoke to Arjuna, "Let him go, brother. There is no greater punishment for a man then getting humiliated in the presence of his wives."

Angaraparva panted shame faced. Arjuna said to him, "Listen Gandharva chief! I forgive you upon the wish of my righteous elder brother."

Angaraparva thanked God and expressed gratitude to Pandavas, "For sparing my life I want to give you a little gift that will make you master of a divine power. It is called 'Chakshusee'. With this power you will be able to see anything, any where in the three worlds any time. It will so empower human pair of eyes. Besides that I gift you 100 Gandharva horses that never grow old and race at the speed you would wish without slowing down."

Pandavas were greatly pleased at such gifts. Arjuna said, "King Angarparva! We accept your gifts as a token of your friendship. We wish to keep gifts with you till we need them in future. We thank you for your kind gifts."

Angarparva promised, "I will always be at your service."

And Angarparva boarded his chariot along with his wives and departed for his divine abode.

❏ ❏

DRAUPADI SWAYAMWARA

During their stay in the forests, Pandavas came to know that Panchala King Drupada was going to hold Swayamwara for the selection of groom for his daughter Draupadi. A group of Brahmins had revealed that. The group itself was going to Panchala in the hope of getting good alms. Pandavas went along. It was willed by Sage Vyasa.

The Brahmins travelling with Pandavas were not aware of their true identity. They took them for some Brahmins. After days of travel they reached Panchala. Pandavas went around the city to see its grandeur. Everywhere they heard the talk of the stunning beauty, charms and the noble qualities of Draupadi.

Then, the appointed day of Swayamwara arrived.

The venue was chock-a-block with kings and princes. And Pandavas went into stand amidst the crowd of Brahmins. They saw the attending kings and princes, all great warriors and one better than the other. Duryodhana and Karna were also there. On one side, sat sages and priests. Krishna and Balrama too had come. Lord Krishna recognised the Pandavas and smiled. King Drupada sat on his throne and was greeting all the incoming guests.

When all had arrived, King Drupada signalled to his son, Dhrishtadhyumana to commence the proceedings. He went in to bring out his sister, Draupadi.

The court announcer announced the arrival of the princess Draupadi.

Draupadi walked with her brother gracefully into the venue. The kings and the princes stared at her spell bound beauty. She was truely drazzling in her finery. She paid obeisance to sages, family guru, her father, Krishna-Balrama and elders before taking her seat.

Then, Dhrishtadhyumana addressed to the guests, "Honourable Royal Persons! As you know it is my sister Draupadi's Swayamwara. My father's vow is that he would give my sister in marriage to the warrior who successfully pierces the eye of the fish that revolves by a spoked wheel on top of the pole with his arrow aimed by looking at its refection being cast in the tub of oil that is placed down by the side of the pole. I invite you all to take part. Whoever prides over his marksmanship must come forward and perform the feat to earn the right of the winner of being garlanded by my sister Draupadi."

Dhrishtadhyumana took his seat.

The trials began. Many kings rose and displayed their skills. Many princes showed the feats of their archery. But no one succeeded in hitting the fish eye. The unsuccessful contestents would go back to their seat to sit with their heads down. Suddenly, Karna rose and walked to the oil tub to take the aim at the fish. Some kings raised an objection, "This contest is open only for blue blooded kings and princes. A weaver's son can't take part in it."

At this, Draupadi looked towards Krishna. He smiled and shook his head. That was a clue. Draupadi rose from her seat and announced, "If the weaver's son has managed to be King of some place and wins the contest, still I won't accept him as my husband."

Karna's body and soul seethed with anger. He looked at the objection raising kings with extreme hatred. Then, his angry eyes fixed on Draupadi. And he walked out of the venue kicking the carpets. Duryodhana wanted to stop him but he was too angry to listen. After Karna's walk out Shishupala, Shalya, Yuyutsu and Jarasandha and others also tried their luck but all of them failed.

This worried King Drupada and Dhrishtadhyumana. All the famed archers had tried and none succeeded. It appeared that the Swayamwara condition would remain unfulfilled.

Some one in the crowd loudly lamented, "Had Arjuna been alive today he would have done it."

This started murmurs about Arjuna and he felt a rush of blood. He could not stop himself from leaving the Brahmin mob and marching towards the bow kept near the oil tub for Swayamwara arrow shooting.

The people looked at him puzzled. A Brahmin from the crowd screamed, "Stop him! That fool will bring shame to entire Brahmin community."

"No! Let him go," another voice pleaded, "Look at his body. He is a match to any prince sitting here. He might bring honour to our community."

The kings and the princes looked at that Brahmin youth utterly puzzled. Meanwhile Arjuna had stringed the bow with ease.

Watching him handle the bow like a man of the martial caste 'Kshatriya' delighted the Brahmins. They all screamed, "Welldone Youngman! Show them that Brahmins are no rabbits."

The sages, who mostly came from Brahmin caste also prayed for Arjuna's success.

King Drupada and Dhrishtadhyumana also wished him to succeed to save the grace of Swayamwara.

As Arjuna prepared to put an arrow to the string, the kings and princes debated if a Brahmin could take part in a contest meant for the warrior race.

Arjuna peered in the tub and took aim above at the revolving fish. The arrow went right into the fish eye. A mixed noise of elated screams, hailings and clappings filled the air. Draupadi looked questioningly at Krishna who nodded his head in approval with a smile. Her face brightened up at this.

The kings and princes took it as an insult to them. How could a begging Brahmin boy marry a princes? They refused to accept Arjuna's shot on the ground that he was no professional warrior. They maintained that his arrow hitting the eye of the fish was just an accident. It was a freak hit, the warriors claimed. Arjuna looked at the mocking kings with contempt. He put another arrow to the bow and shot it in the same way as the condition of Swayamwara demanded. The arrow hit other eye of the fish. It was like a hard slap on the face of the doubting kings.

At a signal from Krishna Draupadi took graceful steps to move to Arjuna and put the winner's garland in his neck. For the kings and princes it was like adding salt to the injury. One of them suggested, "We had been invited here to be insulted like this. Drupada needs to be taught a lesson. Let's kill his son and burn his daughter Draupadi right here." The kings liked the idea. They picked up their arms and ran towards their targets.

How could Arjuna remain silent? He pushed Draupadi behind him and picked up the bow and arrows. The enraged Brahmins also rose in support of Arjuna. They rushed at kings and the princes with their sticks and tridents raising battle cries. Arjuna shouted to them, "Relax brothers. Rest assured that I can single handedly deal with the kings and the princes."

And Arjuna rained arrows at the enemies. Many kings and princes fell down out of their senses.

The kings who were in the rear got so frightened that they ran away.

Yudhishthira, Bheema, Nakula, Sahdeva and Krishna-Balrama pair stood aside smiling. Watching the kings fleeing angered Duryodhana. He called his friend Karna to come back and wage a battle against the rampaging Brahmin young man. On Duryodhana's urgings Karna came forward to challenge Arjuna. But at that moment Arjuna was so charged up that he gave Karna no chance to plan his attack. He stunned Karna with volleys of arrows. Karna admitted, "O brave Brahmin! You really are a warrior. Stop your hand. It is no battle ground. I don't fight a Brahmin with full force. In my knowledge only Arjuna was capable of putting up a challenge to me. But you did. Are you some god in Brahmin disguise?"

"I am no god, Karna. Just an ordinary Brahmin. It is merely the power of my guru who taught me archery. I can use all complex weapons you can think of."

Meanwhile, some kings and princes advanced towards King Drupada to attack. Bheema could not tolerate it. He uprooted a massive piller and came to the defence of Drupda. Shalya advanced to challenge him. Bheema tossed the pillar off to one side. Then, he picked up Shalya with his hands and banged him down against the floor.

It gave goose pimples to the rest of the kings and the princes. They fled. Soon, the venue was clear of the kings and the princes. What a shame for them! They had come like lions and had to flee like Jackals. Arjuna and Bheema moved forward. The people made way for them with frightened respect. Draupadi followed them and the rest of three Pandavas brought up the rear. Pandavas and Draupadi came to the potter's house where they were staying. Mother Kunti was in prayers. The five brothers stopped at the door and called out, "Mother! Look, what we have brought today."

Kunti had her back towards the door, so, she said without bothering to look back, "Whatever it is, share equally among the five of you."

Kunti had thought that her sons had got some delicious food item given by some generous person that day. She was herself on fast.

Draupadi's brother had stealthily followed them to find out the real identity of the warrior Brahmins. He was listening to their talk from a nearby hiding.

When Pandavas were silent not knowing what to say or do, Kunti looked back. She was surprised to find a stunning beauty in royal finery standing beside her sons. Then she remembered her words and regretted them. She explained, "Sons! I am sorry. I thought that you had got some rich food items in alms, so I told you to share it. Who is she?"

Yudhishthira narrated to her all that had happened at Swayamwara and said, "This is the princess Draupadi whose Swayamwara was held. Now she is your daughter-in-law and Arjuna's wife. And you ordered us to share her."

Now Kunti was sad and sorry for her order. It meant polygamy for Draupadi. Kunti looked ashamed of herself and embarrassed to no end. When Draupadi saw Kunti in such painful dilemma, she revealed, "Mother-in-law, you need not worry and feel miserable about it. It is fated for me. I was sent on this earth blessed by gods to have five husbands. That is coming true. I am not worried."

Just then Krishna and Balrama appeared there. They touched feet of Kunti who was related to them as aunt being the sister of their father. Thus, Pandavas and Krishna-Balrama had very close friendly relationship. Krishna revealed that he had recognised Pandavas at the Swayamwara. After the brief meeting Krishna-Balrama went back home.

When Draupadi found out that her Swayamwara winner was none other than Arjuna, she was ecstatic. She realised that she was the wife of the mighty Pandavas and the daughter-in-law of great Kuru dynasty.

Meanwhile, Dhrishtadhyumana found out that the Brahmins were infact Pandavas. He was overjoyed. He had heard everything that went between Kunti and Krishna. Now he could not wait to give the news to his father.

"Father! Don't worry about the fate of Draupadi. The winner of her hand is no mean Brahmin. He is infact a warrior. My sister and your daughter has become the bride of the famous Kuru dynasty of Hastinapur. That Brahmin youngman is infact the valiant prince, Arjuna of Pandavas."

"Arjuna! Pandavas!!" King Drupada was stunned. He could not believe it. "Dhrishtadhyumana! Are you mad? That evil Duryodhana is supposed to have burnt the Pandavas alive in a lac-house. So, what you say is impossible."

"Whatever Duryodhana is supposed to have done is rubbish. The fact is that Pandavas are alive. All of them including Kunti. Even Krishna went to meet them before leaving for his Dwarika. You can see for yourself. They are staying at a potter's house in this very city."

Now, King Drupada had to believe his son. The truth made the King a very happy man. He at once gave orders to prepare for a royal welcome to Pandavas and their mother.

The arrangements for a grand reception began in earnest. Meanwhile, sage Vyasa arrived there. King Drupada touched his feat and got him seated. Then he put his conflict before the sage, "O Great Sage! I am in a dilemma. Please guide me."

"Well, King! What is it?"

"How can my daughter Draupadi accept five men as her husbands? Will it not be against our social and religious norms?"

"King! Stop worrying. It is god willed act. Draupadi is a gift of heavens. While sending her to the mortal world of the earth Lord Shiva had revealed to her that she would marry five grooms."

This cleared all the doubts of the mind of King Drupada. He duly got his daughter married to five Pandavas in a royal ceremony with great fanfare.

❏ ❏

DHRITRASHTRA, DURYODHANA AND KARNA INTERACT

The news of Pandavas being alive and their marriage to Draupadi had reached Hastinapur too. It had shaken Dhritrashtra and Duryodhana. Vidura was getting all the information about Pandavas from his spies. As the news had become public, he thought it to be his duty to inform the King. So, he entered the chamber of the King and said to Dhritrashtra, "It has been confirmed that Pandavas are alive along with Kunti. And the winner of Draupadi swayamwara is indeed Arjuna. Our spies report that Draupadi has been married to five Pandava brothers as willed by Lord Shiva."

"Great!" Dhritrashtra managed to smile. But his forehead showed lines of anxiety and worry.

In the presence of Vidura, Dhritrashtra thanked God million times for saving dear Pandavas and expressed happiness at their wedding with Draupadi. He ordered royal finery and jewellery to be made for them. The King asked Vidura to go to Panchala and bring back Pandavas with due respect and honour.

As soon as Vidura left, Duryodhana and Karna entered. They had heard what went between Dhritrashtra and Vidura. So, Duryodhana was angry. He spoke, "What have you done, fahter? I heard everything. You are sending Vidura to bring back Pandavas?"

"Duryodhana! You are a child. Don't you know that Vidura is well wisher of Pandavas? I had to say those things for his benefit and for our safety. How could I reveal my true feelings to him? We must carry on this act otherwise the supporters of Pandavas will rise against us. Now you tell me what is in your mind?"

"First thing we must do is to finish Bheema," Duryodhana said excitedly and added. "He is the mightiest of them. His death would mean half the power of Pandavas lost. Then the rest will never dare to even think of the Hastinapur throne. And we can turn King Drupada against them. After all, silly words of Kunti led to his daughter Draupadi having to marry five men. Thus, Drupada has been disgraced socially."

"Listen friend," Karna intervened, "What you say about Bheema can be true. But I don't think we can turn Drupada against Pandavas."

"Then suggest something, Karna," Dhritrashtra urged.

"There is only one way. We must attack Panchala at once and defeat King Drupada. Then his son, Pandavas and Kunti should be taken prisoner. That will solve all our problems."

"That is fine," Dhritrashtra remarked blinded by the love for his son and spoke, "Pandavas have already betrayed the people and the throne of Hastinapur by hiding themselves for so many years. They have put the people of the kingdom through great mental torture and agony. So attack on Panchala is justified. But first I must consult Prime Minister Vidura and Grandman Bhishma about it."

GRANDMAN BHISHMA'S REBUKE

King Dhritrashtra was holding court. The ministers were in their respective seats. On one side sat Grandman Bhishma on a special seat. Dhritrashtra put forward his proposal for immediate war against Panchala and he spoke of the follies of Pandavas.

It irked Grandman Bhishma who rose up to say, "It is wrong and should not be carried out. Pandavas are as dear to me as you are. Yudhishthira is now major. So, the throne of his father should be handed over to him. What is the justification of war against Panchala? It is now a known fact that Duryodhana had tried to destroy Pandavas in lac-house with the help of the minister Purochana. We know about it. Pandava's are wandering around hiding themselves to evade the murderous plots of Duryodhana. If Duryodhana does not mend his ways, something ugly will happen. It won't be good."

Dhritrashtra hung his head in shame at receiving the strong rebuke from Bhishma. But he defended his son, "Respected Grandman! Please think kindly about Duryodhana also. He has ambitions like any prince."

The members of the court departed on the issue. At last with the approval of Grandman Bhishma it was decided that the half of the kingdom of Hastinapur be given to Pandavas as a peace deal. Dronacharya and Vidura too supported the decision.

Thus, all the powerful members of the court made it known to Dhritrashtra and Duryodhana that Pandavas had a lot of goodwill and support in the court.

So, Dhritrashtra announced, "I accept your wise decision. After all, Pandava's too are my own dear nephews. Vidura! Go to Panchala and bring home Pandavas and their bride with due royal tradition."

❑ ❑

VIDURA IN PANCHALA

Vidura was given a royal welcome in Panchala. He was put up in the royal guest house. Then, King Drupada requested him to reveal the purpose of his kind visit. Vidura handed to him heaps of costly gifts and informed that they were for the bride Draupadi from the royal members of Kuru dynasty.

Later, Vidura stated the purpose of his arrival, "King! I am here as a representative of King Dhritrashtra, Grandman Bhishma, Guru Dronacharya, female members of the Hastinapur royal palaces and the people of the kingdom. All are overjoyed at the marital alliance between Panchala and Hastinapur. We regret the misdeeds of Duryodhana and wish the return of Pandavas to Hastinapur. Queen Gandhari is eagerly waiting to welcome Draupadi into the family fold. So, kindly allow Pandavas to return to Hastinapur."

Luckily Krishna and Balrama too were present there when the meeting took place. They had arrived in Panchala just a short time before Vidura had done. They heard the request of Vidura. All eyes turned to King Drupada. He thought for a while before speaking, "Respected Vidura! Pandavas are my sons-in-law. It will be impolite of me to ask them to depart espicially when dangers stalk them. Who can guarantee that Duryodhana won't play any mischief again? Still, I will leave the final decision to the wisdom of Krishna and Balrama."

Vidura looked towards Krishna and said, "Lord Krishna! What do you say?"

"I think Pandavas should go to Hastinapur and accept half of their father's kingdom on offer. They should create a new capital for their part of the kingdom and live peacefully. It will help end the enmity between Kauravas and Pandavas."

Pandavas gladly accept the suggestion. The very next day the party of Pandavas, Kunti, Draupadi, Krishna and Vidura set out for Hastinapur.

Pandavas received a rousing reception at Hastinapur. The people were excited and turned out in large numbers to cheer them because for many they were people come alive from dead. Crowds hailed Kunti and her sons. Pandva brothers touched the feet of Grandman Bhishma, King Dhritrashtra, Guru Drona, family priest Kripacharya and other elders to get blessed. Kunti and Draupadi proceeded to the palace of Queen Gandhari. The older women fell in each other's arms and wept. Gandhari sought pardon of Kunti for the misdeeds of Duryodhana. Then, Queen Gandhari hugged Draupadi tightly and caressed her lovingiy. She gave the bride million blessings.

The city went into ruptures. There was rejoicing all over. All citizens believed that Yudhishthira was going to be their King. There were hopes and great expectations.

❏ ❏

THE DIVISION OF KINGDOM PROPOSED TO YUDHISHTHIRA

The next day, Hastinapur court sat in meeting. On the invitation of Grandman Bhishma, Pandavas also attended the meeting. King Dhritrashtra addressed to Yudhishthira, "Son! You are a model of righteousness, wisdom and patience. Being the eldest son of Pandu, the throne of Hastinapur rightly belonged to you. After my brother Pandu's demise I was made caretaker King as you were just a kid. My becoming King aroused a desire in my son to be the next King. So, all the elders of this court have suggested the division of our kingdom. One part for you and the other for Duryodhana so as to maintain the peace and the brotherly love among us and in our family. Son, I hope you will accept the division for the sake of peace in our family. That is the only way to satisfy both of you eldest of the rival groups, we all want you to make Khandwaprastha your capital and live royally."

Yudhishthira was soft and polite by nature. He readily accepted the proposal. It brightened up all the faces. No one had believed that such twisted problem could straighten up so easily. It was historic.

Bhishma, Drona, Kripacharya and Vidura paid tributes to the generosity of Yudhishthira and blessed him.

INDRAPRASTHA COMES UP

Yudhishthira went to Khandwaprastha with his brothers, mother and Draupadi to start a new life. The people of that part heartily

welcomed them. Gradually Khandwaprastha became prosperous with a new capital called Indraprastha where Pandavas lived in splendour in a magnificient palace.

❑ ❑

PANDAVA PACT

One day when Pandava brothers were sitting in court the wandering sage Narada arrived. He had come to give advice to the brothers regarding Draupadi. He narrated the story of two demon brothers named Sund and Upsund who had died fighting over a beauteous woman 'Tillotama'. So, at the wise advice of sage Narada,

Pandava brothers made a pact that each brother would live with Draupadi in turns for a month in each term. During that period no other brother would enter Draupadi's chamber. Any brother violating that rule will go on twelve year exile.

□ □

EXILE FOR ARJUNA

Prosperity reigned Indraprastha. One day, a Brahmin came running to Arjuna to tell him that his cow had been stolen. Arjuna got up to go with him to get the cow back. Suddenly, he remembered that his bow was in Draupadi's chamber. And at that time it was Yudhishthira who was living with Draupadi.

Arjuna was in a fix. He didn't want to turn back the Brahmin helpless who could have put some curse. So, he went in into the chamber of Draupadi to get his bow. Though Yudhishthira and Draupadi was not in the room yet it was violation of the pact. After getting the cow back for the Brahmin, Arjuna returned to the palace. He admitted to the brothers about the violation of the rule by him and got ready to go in exile for twelve years. Yudhishthira, Draupadi and other brothers tried to reason that he had done no wrong as there was no one in the chamber. But Arjuna didn't agree and went into exile.

During exile period Arjuna tracked through forests. In the land of Nagas, the princess of Naga King fell for Arjuna and insisted on marrying him. Her name was Uloopi. Infact, it was Uloopi's para powers that had drawn Arjuna to her area. Arjuna could not reject her love. He married her and spent some years in Naga kingdom. One day, Arjuna expressed his wish to move on. Uloopi gladly accepted his wish. She gave a boon to Arjuna to be protected in water and to enjoy the friendship of all water creatures. She was the goddess of water life.

Arjuna moved on. And his wanderings took him to the court of King Chitravahana. Arjuna introduced himself and the King was delighted to meet the famed archer. He requested Arjuna to stay with him for some time as a royal guest. Arjuna accepted the invitation. One day, princess Chitrangada happened to see Arjuna. She fell madly in love with his manly beauty. She proposed marriage to Arjuna. Arjuna sought the permission of the King to marry his daughter. King agreed to the marriage on one condition that the first son of Chitrangada will remain with the King because he had no son. He wanted a heir to the throne from his own blood.

Arjuna had no objection to it. The marriage followed in royal style.

In due course Chitrangada gave birth to a son. Arjuna handed over his son to King Chitravahana as promised and moved on.

This time he travelled southwards. In the south, in a deep forest he saw some cottages of sages and saints. They gave Arjuna the knowledge of religious wisdom. After blessing Arjuna, the sages revealed that there were five ponds nearby but they could not take water from them. Thus, they were always thirsty for water. When Arjuna wanted to know the reason, he was told that every pond was a home of a big crocodile that gobbled anyone who approached the pond.

Arjuna assured them that he would free them of the terror of crocodiles.

He got into a pond. The crocodile of that pond came at him. But Arjuna was blessed with the boon given by his wife Uloopi to be protected from any harm in water. He fearlessly caught the crocodile by it's tail and flung it out of the water. As soon as the crocodile hit the ground it transformed into a heavenly beauty.

She said, "O son of Pandu! All of the crocodiles in these ponds are angels of heavens. A curse put on us by a sage had turned us into crocodiles. You were to left the curse off us. We have been waiting for you for a hundred years. So, please lift the curse off other crocodiles too."

Arjuna liberated them all and the sages heaved a sigh of relief. The heavenly beauties thanked Arjuna and streaked towards the heavens. The sages blessed him.

Arjuna moved on.

He went north-westwards where he met Krishna in Prabhasa region. Lord Krishna had prior knowledge that Arjuna would descend in his area.

He took Arjuna to his capital city Dwarika where Balrama gave them grand reception. Arjuna started living there.

One day his eyes fell on Subhadra, the virgin sister of Balrama. He at once lost his heart to her. He expressed his wish to Krishna to make Subhadra his wife.

Krishna smiled and said, "Man! warriors don't beg for girls. They take them."

So, egged on by Krishna, one day Arjuna grabbed the hand of Subhadra and took her away with him.

The news enraged Balrama. Krishna advised him, "Brother! You can't win against Arjuna in battle. So, waging a war will be stupid and meaningless. Just think, where shall we find a better groom than warrior Arjuna for our dear sister Subhadra? Let it ride."

Balrama saw merit in his brother's advice. He called Arjuna and Subhadra back in to the city and properly got them married.

Arjuna came to Pushkar with Subhadra and spent the remaining years of exile there.

❑ ❑

ARJUNA RETURNS— ABHIMANYU BORN

At the end of the exile period, Arjuna returned to Indraprastha with Subhadra in the guise of a milk maid. He paid obeisance to his King brother, Yudhishthira. Then, he entered the palace with Subhadra in tow. Upon learning the identity of Subhadra, overjoyed Kunti embraced her and blessed her with wishes of happiness. Subhadra went to meet Draupadi. After paying her respects she appealed to Queen Draupadi, "Elder sister! Give me the honour of being your maid." Her politeness overwhelmed Draupadi who took Subhadra in her arms.

The news of Arjuna's return to Indraprastha reached Dwarika also. Krishna and Balrama arrived at Indraprastha with great many valuable gifts to confirm their sister's marriage to Arjuna. King Yudhishtira on his part organised a great feast to celebrate the union of Arjuna and Subhadra. Sweets and gifts were distributed. Balrama returned to Dwarika after a few days. But Krishna stayed back on the request of Arjuna. They were very fond of each other.

A few weeks hence, Subhadra gave birth to a lovely male child. The priests christened him 'Abhimanyu'. Abhimanyu grew up fast. He was very active and clever. In bravery he showed all signs of being equal to his uncles and father. The entire family was very fond of him and his pranks delighted everyone. Krishna loved the kid very much. At the age of seven, Arjuna began teaching him archery. Bheema trained him in the use of mace. By the time he entered his teens he had already become a warrior. A warrior who could match any great fighter. He was becoming a feared name. Pandavas were very proud of Abhimanyu.

Meanwhile, Draupadi too kept giving birth to sons. She had five sons—Pratibindhya, Shrutkarma, Shrutsena, Sutsena and Shataneeka.

These five princes also grew up alongside Abhimanyu. The family priest, Ayudhomya performed their customary shaving and thread ceremonies. All five progressed towards great manhood which pleased Pandavas and the pride of the family soared.

❑ ❑

THE HUNGER OF FIRE-GOD

Krishna was still in Indraprastha. Staying with the relative and bosom friend Arjuna was pleasure for him.

One day, a strange thing happened. It was hot day of summer. Because of the heat Krishna and Arjuna went to the bank of the river Yamuna and sat down under the shade of a tree. Shortly, a Brahmin appeared there and spoke, "Help me, please."

"Respected Brahmin! say, what can we do for you?"

"I am hungry. I want food. Remember, I need lots and lots of food."

"What do you want in food and how much?" Arjuna asked. The Brahmin shed his disguise to show himself in real form. He spoke, "I am no Brahmin. I am god of fire. I eat fire. I want this Khandawa forest go up in flames for me to eat. But Lord Indra does not let me do it because his friend, the King of snakes, Takshakraj lives in this forest. As soon as I start fire he sends down heavy showers to put out the fire. That's how I have been starving."

Krishna and Arjuna looked at each other.

The fire god added, "Do not hesitate or think over it. I know that you two have incredible divine powers. So, you can help me. You have powers to cut out the showers to let the fire spread and rage. It will feed me nice."

"O Fire-god! We shall use whatever powers we have but we don't have any power to counter Lord Indra. We shall help you if you can get us some such special weapons." Arjuna informed.

At this, the Fire-god invoked Water-god. When the Water-god appeared he asked him to provide weapons which could be used against Indra.

The Water-god produced two bows, two quivers which remained ever full of arrows and two chariots that had red flags.

The Fire-god gave those divine weapons to Arjuna. He also gave a divine disc that had spiked edge to Krishna and revealed, "O Krishna! This is Sudarshan Chakra. With it you can defeat the greatest of the demons and the gods. It will come back to you after slaying the enemy. And take a mace too which can strike like Indra's bolt of lightning."

This happened when Khandawa forests had become home of dacoits and fugitive criminals. They posed a permanent threat to the law and order. The citizens were getting robbed and murdered. To solve that problem Arjuna and Krishna allowed the Fire-god to destroy the forest. In a flash the fire started and engulfed the forest in flames. The Fire-god satisfied his hunger and criminals perished.

❏ ❏

ANGRY INDRA ON WARPATH

The fire in Khandawa forest became so fierce that its flames leapt skywards. The heat of the flames reached the heavens and the gods also felt the heat. Lord Indra was informed that Fire-god had set Khandawa forest on fire. Indra was shocked. He, at once thought of his friend Takshaka. With his divine sight he viewed the Khandawa forest and saw the flames leaping sky high. It enraged him. To help his friend Indra sent down showers. But the fire was so fierce that the showers turned into steam in sky itself.

This added fuel to the fire of the anger of Indra. He invoked the army of gods and set out for Khandawa on his elephant Erawat. He had his thunderbolt 'Vajra' in his hand. Indra was on warpath.

At Khandawa, Krishna and Arjuna stood guard to protect the Fire-god. They were armed with their newly gifted divine weapons. Indra was surprised to see them. He remembered the incident of Gokul where Krishna had defeated him on the issue of the worship of Govardhan mountain. The sight of Krishna and Arjuna frightened other gods who fled off their chariots. But fleeing from battle was against the pride of Indra. It had become a prestige issue for him. He picked up a hill-top and tossed it on Krishna and Arjuna. Arjuna destroyed it with the divine weapons provided by the Water-god.

Indra seethed in anger but before he could launch new attack, a divine voice from the skies announced, "O Indra! The friend for whom you worry and wage this battle has already fled the forest. He is safe and sound. Don't grieve for him. Let the fire of this forest consume demons, fugitives and criminals who have made it their hide out. Seek pardon of Lord Krishna and return to your abode."

This made Indra realise his mistake. He apologized to Krishna and went back to heavens.

❑ ❑

MAYA DEMON'S CREATION

Out of the burning Khandawa forest a demon named Maya came out racing to save his life. The Fire-god saw him and leapt towards him. Maya ran on. He saw Krishna with Sudarshan Chakra blocking his way. He turned and ran towards Arjuna and fell at his feet begging for life. Arjuna asked Fire-god and Krishna to spare the demon. The Fire-god went away after satisfying his hunger. Arjuna sat down with Maya demon under a tree.

Maya thankfully spoke to Arjuna, "O Son of Pandu! I am an expert in building houses with illusion architecture. You have saved my life. In return do ask me to give some service to you."

Krishna suggested, "If that is true, create a great palace for King Yudhishthira of Indraprastha, so unique that no human must be able to build such one."

Maya demon began building the palace for the Pandava King. It was ready in due time.

The palace was a wonder. An amazing creation. The illusion was fantastic. The flowing water gave the impression of being a solid floor with attractive design. What looked like a solid floor would infact be a pool of water. On the flower patterned walls one could see three dimensional doors and windows which were not there in reality. A door would be where it looked like a solid wall. It was a maze of illusions. The decoration was amazing. Walls had flowery patterns made of embedded precious stones. Floors were made of marbles of various shades to create designs.

Pandavas were delighted to have such a palace, the kind of which nowhere else existed on earth. They thanked the illusion artist architect Maya demon. Infact, he was so thankful to Arjuna that he was not satisfied with the gift of that palace. He wanted to give more. Maya insisted on it.

Arjuna gave in. Maya demon brought some amazing gifts from Kailasha mountain, a golden diamond-studded mace for Bheema and a conchshell named Devadutta for Arjuna.

Then, Arjuna gave Maya the protection and the permission to leave for any place of his choice.

The family priest, Ayudhomya performed house-entry customs and the Pandavas began living in that magnificient palace. It took them quite some time, get familiar with the illusions and learn where floors, water, walls, doors and windows really were. The palace indeed was mind boggling.

One day, footloose sage Narada visited Indraprastha. King Yudhishthira got him seated on a highly honoured seat.

The sage said, "King! I have come to inform you about a wish of your father that he had revealed to me. But he could not fulfil it."

"What was the wish, O sage," Yudhishthira asked anxiously.

"Wish to perform Rajsuya Yajna. You must do it for your father."

"I will fulfil the wish of my father, O sage." Then, he consulted Krishna. After being briefed Krishna said, "Of course, you must do it, Yudhishthira. But do one thing before that."

"What is it, Lord Krishna?"

"King! I am afraid that the King of Magadha, Jarasandha will try to obstruct the Yajna. You know that he is deadset against me since I slayed his in-law Kansa. And now I am a part of you. Befor Yajna we must finish off Jarasandha."

"But how will that be possible? I hear that due to a boon by Lord Shiva, he is almost invincible. And he has imprisoned too many kings on false charges who are to be sacrificed to please Rudra-god."

"Don't worry, King," Krishna said and added, "Leave that to me. Just send Bheema and Arjuna with me. I will get him killed by Bheema. The victory over Jarasandha would prove your superiority and your yajna will smoothly go on."

Yudhishthira was not fully convinced. Although he had full faith in Krishna and knew that in his presence no harm would come to his brothers but Jarasandha was no ordinary mortal. He was the mightiest King of the entire North region.

Krishna understood his dilemma. He said, "Don't get worrying like that, King. Whatever will be, will be. The time is all consuming. It claims everyone. The end time of that Jarasandha is coming. The law of nature...King," Krishna smiled mysteriously and remarked, "No one can stay alive when sins cross the limit. Listen to my plan..."

Krishna revealed to Yudhishthira his plan. Then Yudhishthira spoke, "Now I am convinced that under your guidance Bheema will be able to vanquish Jarasandha. And then, invincible archer Arjuna is with you. Our aim is pious. The death of Jarasandha would mean the freedom of the innocent kings whom he plans to sacrifice."

❑ ❑

JARASANDHA SLAIN

As soon as King Yudhishthira gave permission, Krishna departed for Magadha with Arjuna and Bheema. They were in the disguise of Brahmins. Meanwhile, on the advice of his priest, Jarasandha had organised a Yajna to ward off any calamity on his kingdom. The three phoney Brahmins arrived as the yajna was in progress. Taking them for Brahmins, Jarasandha welcomed them. Bheema and Arjuna kept silent but Krishna spoke, "King! My companions are observing silence till midnight tonight. Please excuse them."

"If that is so, you can retire to the guest house, sirs. I will come to talk with you after midnight." Jarasandha got busy in Yajna.

He came to the guest house true to his word just after midnight and paid obeisance. Arjuna and Bheema blessed him as expected and requested him to sit down. After sitting, Jarasandha looked at Bheema and Arjuna hard. He had suspected the intentions of the three. So, he said, "Kindly reveal your identities and tell me the purpose of your visit."

According to the plan of Krishna, Bheema gave his true introduction and challenged Jarasandha for a wrestling bout. Then, Krishna and Arjuna revealed their identities.

The identities of the visitors and the challenge for a bout drove Jarasandha mad with anger. He accepted the challenge.

The day of the bout was fixed for the day after.

Jarasandha said, "I suspected you in the morning itself. There was something unnatural about you. You were in Brahmin guise but walked like warriors. What is the idea of challenging me in my own house?"

"An enemy can be challenged in his house for no reason."

"What makes us enemies?" Jarasandha asked in surprise.

"You have made scores of kings your prisoners. We don't like it because we too are kings."

"To take them prisoners, I defeated them in battles," Jarasandha argued, "Now, as a victor I will do to them whatever I wish."

"That wish thing is alright...", Krishna reasoned, "But you want to sacrifice them before a deity. Is it right for a King to sacrifice another King? It is claimed that you wish to sacrifice 100 kings. You still are short of the hundred figure. It is possible that you might wage a war against us to make up that number. So, we thought it to be safe to challenge you for a wrestling bout to avoid unnecessary bloodshed. Only the winner shall come out alive. If you don't wish to battle against mighty Bheema accept defeat and free all the imprisoned kings."

It further enraged Jarasandha. He controlled himself with difficulty and announced, "I accept the challenge. Say, does Bheema want to fight sword duel, mace charge or wrestling?"

"The wrestling," Bheema replied.

Thus, the wrestling bout was agreed upon. The news spread like wild fire that there would be a great bout between King Jarasandha and Pandava battler Bheema.

The people collected in large numbers to watch the battle.

And at appointed time the bout began. The bout raged on for thirteen days without any result. Both were equally mighty. Neither of them tired or backed out.

It was a titanic battle.

They entered the venue for the fourteenth day's marathon wrestling. Krishna shouted to Bheema to upset Jarasandha, "Bheema! Take pity on your opponent. Don't hit hard. The poor fellow appears to be tired and beaten. Don't use any divine power blessed to you by gods. Spare his life."

It was a clue for Bheema.

He rushed at Jarasandha and picked him up in one mighty jerk up in the air and then raised him above his head to bang him down on the ground.

Krishna plucked a leaf from a nearby tree and tore it in two for the benefit of Bheema who tore Jarasandha in two by tearing apart his legs.

Infact, Jarasandha was born in two vertical parts and a demoness had joined them together. Bheema had torn that seam.

He flung away the parts and looked at Krishna and Arjuna proudly.

Suddenly, he heard the roaring laughter of Jarasandha. Bheema turned back to get a shock. Jarasandha parts had come together and he stood there laughing at Bheema. His eyes were flashing anger.

Bheema stood confused for some time and looked at Krishna questioningly.

Krishna again tore a leaf and threw the parts in the cross directions i.e. left part in right and right part in left direction.

Bheema got it. He again managed to tore Jarasandha apart in a similar move as before. But this time he flung the parts in cross directions. The parts stayed there on the ground dead and still. Bheema's victory gave boundless joy to Krishna and Arjuna.

The frightened people hailed Bheema.

There was wailing and mourning in the palace when the news got there.

Krishna, Arjuna and Bheema went to the palace.

The son of Jarasandha, Sahdeva was scared but he welcomed them. Krishna assured him of his protection and declared him the new King of Magadha.

He was crowned in due ceremony.

Then, on the urgings of Krishna and Arjuna he announced the release of the kings imprisoned by his father. The liberated kings thanked Krishna and Pandava brothers. They paid special tribute to the valour and the might of Bheema.

Bheema gave all the credit of his victory to Krishna and Pandava brothers accepted the thanks and the congratulations of the kings. All the freed kings were requested to attend the Rajsuya Yajna of Yudhishthira.

After accomplishing the task, the trio returned to Hastinapur.

❑ ❑

❖ SHISHUPAL BEHEADED ❖

The death of Jarasandha pleased King Yudhishthira. Then according to the advice of the family priest, he sent invitations for Rajsuya Yajna. All the kings, sages and prominent citizens were requested to take part in it.

Soon, the invitees began arriving. Inderprastha became more and more colourful and dazzling with the royal arrivals. Nakula was sent to Hastinapur. With him came Dhritrashtra, Drona, Vidura, Kripacharya, all the Kaurava princes and Grandman Bhishma. King Dhritrashtra brought valuable gifts for Pandavas, Kunti, Draupadi and Subhadra.

The Yajna duly began with great fanfare and was completed in the care of religious scholars. It was a tradition that at the end of Yajna, a person was chosen from the invited kings and others as the Best Person to be ceremoniously worshipped. Yudhishthira requested the Kings to select their Best Person.

Magadha King, Sahdeva was the first to propose the name of Lord Krishna. Bhishma and Drona seconded the proposal. Many kings also supported the proposal. But some kings objected to it.

They thought that Grandman Bhishma or Drona were more worthy persons. The opposition was led by Shishupal who incidently was a cousin brother of Krishna. He was the son of the sister of Krishna's father. He always hated Krishna and spoke ill of him. Lord Krishna's popularity, charisma and divine powers made him feel extremely jealous. The honour of 'Best Person' going to Krishna was simply intolerable to him. So he rose and aired his opposition, "O King Yudhishthira! King Sahdeva of Magada has proposed Krishna's name not because of his merit but for the reason that he is obliged to Krishna. Sahdeva is stooge of Krishna. Bhishma and Drona too are partial to Krishna. The fact is that Krishna is younger than most of the great people gathered here. How can such immature person deserve this honour?" Then he looked at Krishna and screamed," And You Krishna! Won't you feel ashamed at letting yourself be worshipped in the presence of so many elder and better persons than you are? Yudhishthira and his brothers are afraid of you. But I and many other kings are not afraid of you and are not impressed of you. You should have yourself opposed when your name was proposed. But you did nothing and proved how shameless and mannerless you are."

Shishupal went on spewing venom. He said many unpleasant things and became abusive. But Krishna silently kept smiling.

No one was stopping Shishupal nor shouting him down. So, he thought that others were supporting whatever he was saying. As he spoke on, he became more and more abusive, encouraged by the silence of others. At last Bhishma lost his temper and he rebuked Shishupal. He said to the kings, "You know that among Brahmins, the scholar and among warriors, the most valiant is worshippable. As far as I think Krishna has both these qualities. His knowledge of religions, the political wisdom and valour is recognised by all. He is indeed a character worth worshipping. Shishupal has said so many abusive rubbish but Krishna didn't hit back. Such tolerance alone is worshippable. Shishupal is stupid. He does not know Krishna, inspite of being a close relative. What pity! I warn him not to degrade this solemn occasion by using abusive language."

It infuriated Shishupal who shrieked like a mad person. "I think due to old age Bhishma has gone senile. He is talking like a lackey. Krishna is just a silly cowherd. Stupid people like Bhishma have made a big thing out of him. We know he is nothing. So, we shall not allow him to be treated as the Best Person. It will be an insult to us all."

When Shishupal said ugly things about Grandman Bhishma, Krishna could not keep quiet. He addressed to the gathering, "Honourable guests! You all know that Shishupal is my cousin brother. I can't understand why he is so jealous of me. He has done thousand wrongs to me and countless misdeeds. In my absence he even tried to set fire to my capital Dwarika. I tried to punish him several times but every time his mother, who is my dear aunt begged me to forgive him. I promised her that I would forgive his 100 misdeeds. He crossed that limit long ago but I tolerated. But the way he today insulted our respected Grandman Bhishma, he has crossed all limits and does not deserve any mercy. I will punish him."

Saying this, Krishna released his Sudarshan Chakra at Shishupal. Shishupal tried to run away but failed. The Sudarshan Chakra sliced through his neck beheading him and it returned to Krishna.

His fate frightened the kings who were supporting him but Krishna forgave them.

❏ ❏

DRAUPADI'S TAUNT

The killing of Shishupal created some unpleastantness in the religious ceremony but Krishna cleverly controlled the damage and the situation became normal. King Yudhishthira gave suitable gifts to all the kings and the relatives and saw them off. But Duryodhana was so mesmerized by the wonders of Yudhishthira's palace that he expressed his wish to stay there with his uncle Shakuni for some more days.

Everything about that palace built by Maya demon was like a jigsaw puzzle. There, a wall looked like a gate, a door looked like a wall, the solid flour gave the impression of flowing water and what looked like a pool turned out to be a solid floor. Duryodhana was enjoying it.

And this fancy sowed the seeds of a great destruction. Once, Duryodhana and Shakuni tried to go through a door which infact was a wall. They crashed against it. Draupadi happened to be in an overlooking chamber inclined on a bed. She laughed derisively and remarked aloud, "Blind son like blind father!"

Draupadi's remark deeply hurt Duryodhana. The words felt like red hot irons branding his body. He thought that Draupadi had deliberately insulted him. He made up his mind to take revenge for the insult.

Only a little later, Duryodhana again made a fool of himself. He walked across a floor with his loin pulled up to the knees because the floor gave the impression of being a water channel. He wondered at the illusion architecture of the palace. Then Duryodhana fell into a pool which had appeared like a beautiful solid floor.

All the inmates of the palace who saw it laughed and made fun of Duryodhana.

He felt greatly insulted and the prosperity of Pandavas turned him green with envy. He spoke to his cunning uncle Shakuni, "Uncle! I just can't tolerate the riches of Pandavas. I have a mind to wage a war against Pandavas and take away their kingdom and this palace."

But crafty Shakuni cautioned Duryodhana and made it clear that defeating Pandavas in a war was impossible task. He advised, "Nephew! with a little craft and cunning you can win everything Pandavas have, including Draupadi who insulted you."

"How, how can I?" Duryodhana asked impatiently, "Is it really possible?"

"Listen nephew! Yudhishthira has gambling habit. That is his weekness. And I never lose in gamble because I can throw mantra loaded dice. Once we are back in Hastinapur, invite Yudhishthira for a gambling session. Leave the rest to me."

❏ ❏

DHRITRASHTRA ALLOWS GAMBLING MATCH

Duryodhana returned to Hastinapur on the same day. He met Dhritrashtra and told him about the great palace of illusions Pandavas had built. Then, he narrated how Draupadi had taunted him. Signs of

anger, showed on the King's face. It encouraged Duryodhana. The iron was hot and he must strike. He hoped that the wish of taking revenge would make Dhritrashtra allow the gambling match to take place as an approved sporting event to make its results legal. So, he said, "Father! I have made a plan with the help of uncle Shakuni to take revenge for our insult. Uncle Shakuni is a wizard at rolling the dice. If we invite Yudhishthira for a gambling session I am sure we can win their palace and everything they have got including the half of the kingdom we gave them and Draupadi too who had the cheek to insult us. I want to see that arrogant woman who called you blind serving as a maid in our palace."

Duryodhana again and again repeated the taunt of Draupadi to fuel the anger of Dhritrashtra. It worked. The King saw merit in Duryodhana's scheme. They would get back the lost part of the kingdom without shedding any blood. He asked Duryodhana to seek advice of Vidura.

Vidura was patiently listening to the dialogue of the King and his son. He advised King Dhritrashtra not to pay heed to Duryodhana and asked Duryodhana to stop hatching evil schemes. A dishonest act can sow the seeds of strife and shall ruin the peace of the both sides, he warned. And Vidura left the meeting.

So, the King did not give permission to Duryodana for his gambling plan.

Duryodhana was disappointed but he did not give up hope. To keep up the pressure he spoke, "Father! Don't get misled by Vidura's talk. He is trying to frighten you off. An enemy must be destroyed by whatever means. Imagine, the same Pandavas who had been running around like beggars for so many years have today become so arrogant as to insult us. Only because we took pity on them and gave half the Kingdon. It has gone to their heads."

"What you say is right, son. But gambling is no good. It leads to ruin. No gambler has ever prospered. It will destroy us. Forget about your gambling scheme and enjoy the princely life." Dhritrashtra reasoned · with his son.

But evil minded Duryodhna refused to understand and insisted on his plan.

Dhritrashtra was too fond of his son to resist for long.

Like always he gave in to Duryodhana. The handicapped Dhritrashtra was not a strong character.

He gave his approval for a dice gambling session between Kauravas and Pandavas to be held in the court of Hastinapur to be witnessed by all the members of court.

A royal order was issued and Vidura had to go to Indraprastha to invite Pandavas.

At Indraprastha, Vidura gave Yudhishthira the royal invitation for a Dice Gambling Match at Hastinapur. Then, at personal level, he advised Yudhishthira against gambling.

But fate had other plans.

Yudhishthira was addicted to gambling. He could not resist any opportunity of gambling. So, he departed for Hastinapur to gamble along with his brothers and Draupadi.

❏ ❏

PANDAVAS IN HASTINAPUR

Shakuni and Duryodhana gave a hearty welcome to Pandavas. After a regal feast, they took rest.

The next day, Dice gambling roll was laid out in the royal court. On one side sat Pandavas and on the other Kaurava party. Shakuni and Karna were the special members of Kaurava team. On behalf of Kauravas, Shakuni spoke, "King Yudhishthira! First, let us set the rules for the game and the stakes etc."

"Yes. The first rule, dear uncle, should be that there should be no cheating," Yudhishthira remarked.

It made Shakuni turn red. He knew that the remark was meant for him. So, he said annoyed, "King! This is gambling. The dice decides everything. There is no scope for any cheating. Every roll of dice will make one winner or loser of whatever the stake. If you dare, come and play. Accept the result sportingly. Or you can refuse to play. There should be no crying later."

"Dear uncle! Don't get upset. Now, tell me who plays and who throws the dice?" Yudhishthira wanted to know.

The reply came from Duryodhana, "I will put the stakes and uncle Shakuni will roll the dice on my behalf. Do you agree to it, dear brother?"

Yudhishthira agreed to it and the game began.

The dice game was being watched by Grandman Bhishma, Dronacharya, Kripacharya, ministers and other prominent courtiers. Dhritrashitra sat on his throne.

Shakuni rolled the loaded dice. Yudishthira lost first stake. The trend continued. Yudhishthira was losing stake after stake. Gradually he lost his wealth, property, kingdom, servants and he staked himself and lost. At last he staked Draupadi and lost her.

Duryodhana was elated. He had successfully plotted the destruction of Pandavas. He was overjoyed when he regained half of the kingdom that was given to Pandavas.

He was guffawing vulgarly like a mad man. Pandavas sat with their heads bent down.

Victory drunk Duryodhana arrogantly ordered Vidura to go to the palace and bring Draupadi to him. He announced that Draupadi would work as a maid servant in his palace.

Vidura said, "Prince Duryodhana! The win at dice has made you forget the basic manners and values. The lady who you talk about is your respected sister-in-law. Have you fallen so low! You are making your own trouble and ruin. To me you look like a deer who is walking into the den of lions."

"Vidura! Don't forget that you are our servant. We made you Prime Minister inspite of the fact that you were a son of a maid because grandman Bhishma recommended you. I am the Crown Prince. How dare you disobey me? Carry out my order or quit."

"Right. I am quitting," Vidura answered, "I always wished the good of Hastinapur and worked for it. But now it appears that my services are no more needed here." And Vidura walked out. Dhritrashtra didn't intervene.

After Vidura's departure, Duryodhana said to his brother Dushasana, "You go and do it. Drag her here. Tell Draupadi that she is no more the Queen of Indraprastha, but our maid."

Dushasana marched to the chamber of the guest house where Draupadi was resting. He stood and leered at her shamelessly. He laughed rudely which surprised Draupadi. She asked, "What's the matter, Dushasana? How dare you enter my chamber without seeking my permission?"

"No permission from a maid is required, Draupadi. Your husband Yudhishthira has lost you in gamble. He lost everything, his kingdom, his brothers and himself even. You are now our maid. I am ordered to drag you to the court. Are you coming on your own or do I drag you to the court by your hair?"

It shocked Draupadi. She felt a chill. Dushasana had evil all over his face and his eyes sparkled devilishly. Draupadi dashed out of the chamber and ran towards the palace of Queen Gandhari.

But, Dushasana was able to grab her. He caught her by her hair and dragged Draupadi towards the court saying, "Arrogant woman! We have won you in gamble and you are now our property."

Draupadi's hair has loosened open when she got dragged to the court. Her clothes had become untidy. She looked towards Pandavas with tears in her eyes and the eyebrows arched in anger. Pandavas dared not meet her eyes. They stared at the floor in utter shame.

She spat words with great hatred, "Fie on the sons of the dynasty of King Bharata who are wallowing in the lowly acts like gambling forgetting their royal duties! So have they degraded themselves that they don't feel any shame in putting the honour of their women at stake! Fie on these so called elders who sit frozen and watch the daughters of their family getting disgraced in their presence. Will any one tell me, how had a husband who had already lost himself any right to stake his wife?"

No one spoke. There was a pindrop silence in the court. The elders to whom Draupadi had posed the question had no answer. All those famed for valour and bravery sat petrified. it was a great tragedy.

Then, Karna's said, "Duryodhana! Take off all the royal dresses of Pandavas, and their ornaments. Bare the arrogant Draupadi naked."

Dushasana got hold of the corner of Draupadi's saree and began pulling it. He was trying to disrobe her. Draupadi realised that no one present there would come to her help. So, she invoked Lord Krishna silently.

Krishna had arrived there in invisible form. He was helping Draupadi with his divine powers.

Dushasana was pulling off saree but the end was not coming. It was as if Draupadi had a series of thousands of sarees on her with no end in sight. Soon there was mountainous heap of sarees of miriad designs and now reeling off Draupadi. Dushasana was perspiring and looking dead tired and frustrated. He huffed and puffed.

Suddenly, there was total darkness. The clouds rumbled and lightning flashed. A divine voice thundered, "Evil Dushasana! Stop your disgraceful act. Let go of saree and run or lightning will strike you to turn you into ashes."

It frightened Dushasana. He fled forgetting about the saree.

Then, Duryodhana thumped his thigh and said to Draupadi, "Come! Sit on my thigh and let me take revenge on you for calling me the blind son of a blind father."

Bheema could not take it. He rose up and thundered shaking with anger, "Listen Duryodhana! I take a vow that in the battle I shall smash your thigh with my mace. And I will tear open the chest of Dushasana to collect blood for washing the hair of Draupadi."

All these happenings terrified Dhritrashtra. He lost no time in cancelling the gambling result and restoring everything to Pandavas.

❏ ❏

DURYODHANA'S ANGUISH

After getting everything back what they had lost in gamble, Pandavas returned to Indraprastha. Bheema's vow had given shivers to Dhritrashtra who tried to control the situation by nullifying the gamble. But Duryodhana and Dushasana were bitter about it. Dushasana had his own worries. He sensed that Bheema would one day honour his vow at his cost. Dushasana lived in terror of Bheema ever since. He could not sleep properly because Bheema had become a nightmare for him. He was restless.

At last, he ran to Duryodhana and said, "Brother! Father spoiled the entire game. The winings are gone and Draupadi too. And Pandavas have now become our sworn enemies. My heart tells me that they will take revenge on us. Remember the horrible things Bheema said!"

Duryodhana was already ruing the action of their father. He grimly nodded his head as he realised the dangers of Bheema's threats. Suddenly, he got up and walked into the chamber of Dhritrashtra. He was sitting with Gandhari. Gandhari had just expressed her unhappiness over the treatment meted out to Draupadi and Pandavas. Duryodhana appeared followed by Dushasana.

Duryodhana exploded, "Father! You have returned our winnings to Pandavas and messed up everything. You know that we can't tackle them by use of force but still you..." He was shaking. Then, he announced, "But I won't let the half of the kingdom given to Pandavas remain with them. All of Hastinapur belongs to us. Pandu was made the King temporarily because of your blindness. Infact, the throne rightly belongs to us. We can take it back only through some tricks."

It has already been stated that Drithrashtra had blind love for his son. He just remained silent, giving free hand to his son to do anything he wished.

Gandhari said, "Arya! You are indulging your son too much and inviting troubles. Your son will destroy our entire dynasty. Whenever he comes to you with some devilish plan you must reject it firmly. He is taking advantage of your softness. I am afraid that future generations will hold you responsible for the ruin of Kauravas."

"Dear Gandhari! Whatever will be, will be. How can I forget that the crown was passed on to my younger brother ignoring my claim to it? That was the first insult to me. After the death of Pandu I was made the King although I was still blind. The crown belonged to me. Duryodhana is doing no wrong. If the dynasty perishes what can I do? I can't kill the ambitions of my son." Dhritrashtra spoke dryly.

Gandhari fell silent. She could only imagine the horrors of future and shudder.

❏ ❏

YUDHISHTHIRA INVITED FOR RE-MATCH

It was a custom of those days that gamblers were supposed to honour an invitation for dice session. Duryodhana took advantage of it. He sent an invitation to Yudhishthira for repeat gambling match.

This time, Duryodhana proposed a strange condition for stakes. The condition was that the loser would go into a thirteen year exile in wilds. The thirteenth year was to be secret during which the exilee must be untraceable. If located, the exilee would again go into further twelve year exile.

Many well wishers advised Yudhishthira not to repeat the mistake again. But gambling was an irresistible temptation for him. He fell for it mindlessly. The game began just like before.

Shakuni was again rolling loaded dice. Yudhishthira lost again.

Duryodhana and Dushasana were overjoyed. They taunted Pandavas as born losers. Then, Bheema spoke angrily, "Brainless Duryodhana! Listen to my words carefully. The day is not far when I will smash off the heads of you and Dushasana with my mace to kick around. And Arjuna will slay Karna. Our Sahdeva will claim Shakuni, Yes, thirteen years don't take long to pass by."

❑ ❑

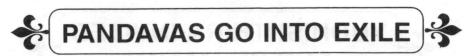

PANDAVAS GO INTO EXILE

As losers in the gamble, Pandavas had to proceed at once for the wilds for thirteen years. Kunti was too weak to face hardships of the exile even for a day. Vidura kindly took her to his home.

Subhadra, Abhimanyu and the five sons of Draupadi departed for Dwarika to stay in the care of Krishna.

Pandava brothers and Draupadi set out for the wilds.

Draupadi's hair hung loose. She had taken a vow that she would not comb or tide her hair until she washed it with the blood of Dushashana.

When Pandavas left Indraprastha, thousands of citizens accompanied them. They felt that the reign of Dhritrashtra-Duryodhana would be like a hell.

Most of the women were also worried about future. When even Bhishma and Drona could not protect the honour of a queen, there appeared no safety of honour in that kingdom.

Many thought that the horrors their kingdom was going through was the result of scheming rascals like Shakuni. Living in a kingdom where such plotters were running loose was dangerous, they said.

When Pandavas found a huge crowd following them, Yudhishthira wanted to know the reason. A person came forward to say, "King! we shall stay with you. We don't want to live in a kingdom ruled by evil persons like Duryodhana and Shakuni. We know that you have been tricked in the gambling. The dice Shakuni rolled was mantra loaded. Allow us to come with you."

The love of the people overwhelmed Yudhishthira.

He said in choked voice, "Brothers! We are grateful for your love and support. Don't forget that our well wishers Grandman Bhishma, Guru Drona, Vidura and our mother also are here. Please take care of them. They are sad at what has happend with us. Don't worry about us, we are on the path of the truth. God is where the turth is. He will protect us."

Thus, Pandavas succeeded in sending the people back to their homes.

Then, Pandavas and Draupadi entered the forests. The family priest of Pandavas, sage Ayudhomya had also learnt about the exile of Pandavas. He too had decided to stay with Pandavas in exile.

In the deep forests, Pandavas built a cottage and began the exile term life there. Sage Ayudhomya raised a hut for himself nearby.

❏ ❏

PROPHECY OF NARADA

Shortly after the departure of Pandavas from Hastinapur, sage Narada arrived in Dhritrashtra's court. He said to the king, "King Dhritrashtra! I have come to inform you that whatever you allowed to happen was no good. You will repent when at the end of thirteen years. Kaurava dynasty will perish and Pandavas shall emerge victorious."

Narada's prophecies always came true. Dhritrashtra and the courtiers were stunned. Dhritrashtra left the court terror struck.

YUDHISHTHIRA PRAYS TO SUN GOD

On the of advice of the family priest, Pandavas had started worshipping Sun-god.

Yudhishthira's devotion pleased the Sun-god. One day when Yudhishthira was offering prayers standing in the river water, the Sun-god appeared in person and spoke, "Yudhishthira! I am pleased. Ask for any boon."

Yudhishthira prayed, "O god! Bless me with the capability of being the provider of my brothers, Draupadi and guests ever."

"So be it," said Sun-god and handed Yudhishthira a pot with advice, "Take it and give it to Draupadi. It will produce any desired food every day, both times in any quantity till Draupadi takes her own meals."

The boon of the Sun-god delighted Draupadi. She respectfully put the pot to her forehead and went inside.

From that day on, Draupadi would feed guests, Brahmins, Pandavas and then she would sit down to take her meals.

❏❏

KRISHNA AND VYASA VISIT PANDAVAS

When Subhadra, Abhimanyu and the sons of Draupadi reached Dwarika, Krishna came to know of the developments. He went to meet Pandavas along with King Drupada. Both of them consoled Pandavas.

Sage Vyasa also came and gave his moral support and the benefit of his wisdom. He predicted, "I can see with my divine sight that you shall fight a great war against Kauravas after thirteen years. Horrible war it will be. You must prepare for it right from now. Do penance and attain divine weapons as many as you can." He said to Arjuna, "Arjuna! You must go to Kailasha mountain and do penance to please Lord Shiva to get blessed with divine bows and arrows."

Arjuna at once got ready to depart for Kailasha mount. Draupadi wished to him, "Dear! I pray for your success with gods, angels and other divine powers. Our good wishes are with you."

ARJUNA ON MOUNT KAILASHA

After taking leave of his brothers and Draupadi, Arjuna set out for Himalayas. Arjuna was master of a knowledge called 'Sidhhasta' which enabled one to teleport oneself by thought. He reached the foothills of Himalayas in no time. He crossed a hill called Gandhamardana and reached Indrakeel mountain.

He was about to move ahead when he heard a harsh voice, "Stop! Don't move ahead."

Arjuna turned his head towards the source of the voice. He saw an aged sage meditating under a tree.

Noticing the bow and arrow in Arjuna's hands the sage asked, "Who are you and why do you wander around with bow and arrows?"

Arjuna bowed his head in respect and replied, "O Sage! I am Arjuna, the son of late King Pandu of Hastinapur."

Sage advised, "This is the area of sages and saints. There is no place for wars or violence here. Throw away your weapons. They are not desired here."

Arjuna was in a fix. Should he do it or not?

Noticing Arjuna's confusion, sage spoke, "Arjuna! I am Indra. Pay attention. Ask any boon from me. Ask and you will get."

Upon learning the identity of the sage, Arjuna got excited. He bowed his head again and prayed. "O Lord Indra! I came here to learn the secrets of divine weapons. Just bless me to be successful in my mission."

"Dear Arjuna! No one here will give you knowledge of divine weapons until you don't do penance to make the Lord of the Lords, Shiva appear to you. Go to the mount Kailasha and meditate to please him. Once you do that I will give all the secret knowledge of divine weapons."

Accordingly, Arjuna reached on Kailasha and sat down on a large rock to begin his penance.

His penance frightened the sages and saints who lived on Kailasha. They went to Lord Shiva in a group and complained, "O Lord of Lords! Open your eyes and see what wrong is taking place here. An ordinary human has come here and he does penance. He is performing Yajna too polluting the air with smoke. It is greatly troubling us. Please do something."

Shiva opened his eyes and assured them, "Don't worry. We know all. He is Arjuna, the son of Pandu, blessed to his wife Kunti by Indra. He is not here to stay for long. He is here on some purpose and with my permission he will leave. His mission is to receive my blessings so that Indra imparts the knowledges of weapons to him."

After learning about Arjuna, the sages and saints returned satisfied and happy.

Then, Lord Shiva transformed himself into a hunter and with Parvati as hunter's wife, came to the spot where Arjuna meditated. He was accompanied by scores of his soldiers and the followers. When they reached there, they found a demon called Mooka advancing at Arjuna in the form of a fiery wild boar. Its grunts disturbed the meditation of Arjuna who opened his eyes and saw the offender.

The aggressive charge of the boar angered Arjuna. He picked up his bow.

Meanwhile, Shiva who was in hunter guise also shot his arrow. So did Arjuna. The two arrows went into the boar at the same time. Arjuna ran to the dead boar and found another arrow too in the kill. He got angry and screamed, "Who dares to shoot arrow at my prey? Show yourself. Don't you know who I am? I am the son of the valiant king, Pandu of Hastinapur."

Shiva as the hunter come from behind a tree to stand before Arjuna challengingly. He harshly claimed, "I was the one who shot arrow first that killed this boar. It belongs to me."

It enraged Arjuna and he said angrily, "So you are the one who shot at my kill. And still you claim that it belongs to you! That is a crime. Warriors don't eye the prey of others. So, you are not a warrior but a thief. I must teach you a lesson." Arjuna started raining arrows at the hunter.

The hunter alias Shiva countered the arrows. It went on for quite some time. Arjuna felt tired. Then he spoke to the hunter, "O Valiant One! Who are you and why do you roam about with your wife?"

"That means that you have accepted defeat, son. You should not pride over yourself so much. The real brave are polite. You are courageous but an inexperienced archer. Go and play with toys for some more years."

Arjuna controlled his anger and said, "You hunter! You have a big mouth. Wait. Let me finish the meditation of Lord Shiva, then I will deal with you."

Arjuna put his bow aside and built up a lingam of snow, the symbol of Lord Shiva. Then, he sat down to meditate with great devotion. After worship he placed a garland of wild flowers around Shivalingam.

When he raised his head, to his surprise he found the garland around the neck of the hunter standing there. Arjuna at once realised that the hunter was infact Lord Shiva himself. He sat at his feet and prayed with folded hands, "O Lord! I was too stupid to see who you were. Kindly forgive my mistakes and my arrogant talk. Blessed am I to find myself in your divine presence. O Lord, you are omniscient. So, you must know why I have come here. God! Show me your real form."

Lord Shiva transformed into his real form and blessed Arjuna, "Son! I am pleased to see your bravery. Your devotion and faith in me is true. So, I bless you with divine wisdom and victory over your enemies in war."

Lord Shiva asked Arjuna what boon he wished for. Arjuna prayed with folded hands, "O Lord of Lords! Please grant me your mightiest weapon 'Pashupatastra' if you really consider me deserving. The weapon which shoots thousands of arrows, maces and spears at enemy simultaneously."

"So be it," Lord Shiva spoke and gave the weapon to Arjuna and warned, "Here it is, son. But use it only when you must. Don't use it for any show. It has the power to destroy the cosmos."

And Lord Shiva told Arjuna that the gods would give him their divine weapons on their own. Then, the Lord disappeared with Parvati and others.

Immediatily after, gods appeared. Arjuna was overwhelmed. The gods blessed Arjuna with their divine weapons and told him the secrets of those weapons.

The success of his mission delighted Arjuna.

Then, Indra spoke, "O Valiant Pandava! You have spent a lot of time at this sacred place with Lord Shiva and the gods. Now it is necessary for you to do some religious deeds."

Indra told him that shortly a divine chariot would come there to take him to Amravati, the capital of Lord Indra of heavenly kingdom. It did and Arjuna boarded it.

The chariot took him to Amravati, there heavenly beauties escorted Arjuna to the court. Lord Indra gave him hearty reception.

In Amravati, Arjuna learnt music and dance from Gandharva King, Chitrasena.

Arjuna stayed there for five years. But Arjuna was tied to the earth and he often remembered his brothers and Draupadi.

Once, the chief courtesan of heaven, Urvashi entered his room and stood by his bed.

The realisation of her presence brought Arjuna out of his thoughts. Greatly surprised, he got off his bed and prayed with folded hands, "Mother! you could have easily summoned me to your presence."

"Dear Arjuna! Don't put me off. A courtesan is no one's mother or sister," she said eying Arjuna coquetishly and added, "The desire for love brings me here. come, let us have fun."

It shocked Arjuna. He pleaded, "What are you saying, lady? You are my respected elder woman. You may be blessed to stay forever young but our earthly relationships are different. You have been wife of the sage who happens to be our guru. I can't even think of having any romantic relationship with you. Kindly bless me to be prosperous, happy and wise."

The courtesan Urvashi tried to win over Arjuna by vulgar gestures and postures but he remained unimpressed. Arjuna was a man of strong will. He didn't give in. This angered Urvashi. She thought that Arjuna had insulted her beauty. So, she put a curse, "Arjuna! You have disappointed me like an impotent man. Hence, for one year, you shall live as an eunuch among beautiful girls and women."

Urvashi was angry but at the same time she was impressed with self control shown by Arjuna. So, she gave a boon too," That year my curse will prove a blessing in disguise for you. It will help you successfully go through the period of the secret exile."

❑ ❑

YUDHISHTHIRA WORRIED FOR ARJUNA

On the other side, when Pandavas didn't get any news of Arjuna even after five years, they got worrying. Draupadi and the four Pandava brothers were fearing the worst. They were imagining lot of dreadful things that could happen to Arjuna. Yudhishthira was cursing himself for putting his brothers and Draupadi in such troubles and hardships. He had become a sad man.

One day, sage Lomesh paid a visit to Pandava cottage, He had learnt a lot about Arjuna's activities through his divine sight. And he knew that Pandavas were very worried about him. So, he gave Pandavas and Draupadi the news of the well being of Arjuna.

Sage said that Arjuna would return after some more time.

Arjuna's success in getting divine weapons from gods pleased Yudhishthira.

Yudishthira requested sage Lomesh to lead them on a pilgrimage. He led Pandavas and Draupadi on pilgrimage and they reached Badrikasharma where the group decided to stay for some time.

BHEEMA MEETS HANUMANA

For some time Pandavas stayed at Badrikasharma. They hoped that Arjuna would come to that place because the place was on the route to Kailasha.

One day, Draupadi and Bheema were sitting on the river bank enjoying the scenery. Draupadi saw a beautiful lily flower being carried down by the river. Draupadi picked it out of the water and spoke to Bheema, "Dear! Look, how beautiful it is! I would like to present it to Yudhishthira. But a single flower would look odd. Some more like it would make a cute gift. Can't you get more for me?"

"Why not? You can go to the cottage. I will look for lilies."

Bheema walked along the bank upstream to find the place where such lilies grew and Draupadi went back home. After walking a long way Bheema reached Gandharmardana hill. The hill was very scenic. On the slopes grew banana groves laden with banana bunches. The waterfalls presented a pretty sight. But Bheema couldn't locate the spot where lilies grew. Then a huge monkey came in the way as a hurdle. His long tree trunk like tail was spread across the path like a series of barriers. Bheema thought it impolite to jump over the tail. So, he stomped his foot on the ground to wake up the monkey. But the monkey opened his eyes and then closed them ignoring Bheema. An angry Bheema thundered, "Stupid monkey! Move out of my way."

The monkey pleaded, "Brother! I am a sick monkey. You can move my tail aside kindly and go your way."

Bheema bent down to fling away the tail of the monkey. But got a surprise. He could not even move the tail a bit. He tried again with both hands but the tail was too heavey to be moved. He wiped away his sweat.

He stood wondering. Bheema had the power of thousand elephants. What happened to that? Why? Suddenly he realised that the monkey was no ordinary creature. It had got to be some divine power in disguise. So, Bheema folded his hands and prayed to the monkey, "O Mighty One! I, the son of Pandu, named Bheema pay respects to you. And I beg you to give me your true introduction."

The monkey rose up and turned into Hanumana. He embraced Bheema and said, "Bheema! I am Hanumana. I am your elder brother since we both are the blessings of Wind-god."

Hanumana's revelation delighted Bheema. He formally paid obeisance to his respected elder brother. Hanumana blessed his younger brother, "Bheema! I will always be with you in every battle to frighten your enemies."

"Brother! I am blessed to have your good wishes. At this point I have only one enemy on earth and that is Duryodhana."

Hanumana directed him towards the Kubera garden on the Sungandik mountain where those lilies blossomed. He thanked Hanumana and moved ahead. Kubera garden pleased him. The lilies grew in a lake of the garden. Bheema tried to pluck a lily when a guard stopped him, "Beware! Don't touch those flowers."

Bheema didn't like it. Somehow, he controlled his anger and said, "I didn't come here to do any damage to the garden. I want only a few flowers. Kindly allow me to take some."

"Shut up! Who are you to invade this area of gods?"

"I am the son of King Pandu of Hastinapur. I want a few flowers for my brother. A few flowers are not going to ruin your garden." He said.

But the guard started rebuking Bheema. Bheema raised his mace and challenged the guard. Many guards pounced on Bheema who swung his mace and sent down most of them. Some guards ran away to Kubera. After learning about Bheema, Kubera asked his guards to let him take the flowers.

Bheema returned with a load of lilies. He gave the flowers to Draupadi who presented them to Yudhishthira.

❏ ❏

ARJUNA'S RETURN

Pandavas anxiously waited for the return of Arjuna. One day the wait ended. Pandava brothers and Draupadi were sitting outside their cottage when they saw a divine chariot descend from the skies. And the person to alight from the chariot was Arjuna.

Arjuna had brought a load of divine weapons, jewellery and divine gifts. He handed over everything to Draupadi except the weapons. Arjuna narrated the story of his journeys.

Yudhishthira was so excited to see the divine weapons that he asked for a demonstration of their powers. Arjuna at once agreed to show them the works.

Just then, sage Narada appeared there. He coutioned, "Arjuna! Remember Lord Shiva's warning not to use these weapons for non-serious reason or the cosmos will get destroyed?"

Arjuna at once realised his mistake. He thanked Narada for averting the disaster he was foolishly going to bring.

Meanwhile in Hastinapur, one day Dhritrashtra was holding court. The ministers, chieftans and Shakuni was also there. A Brahmin arrived in the court. King Dhritrashtra welcomed him and got him seated on a high seat. In talks the Brahmin revealed that he had seen Pandavas in the forests and that they were facing extreme hardships. Dhritrashtra was very pained to hear this.

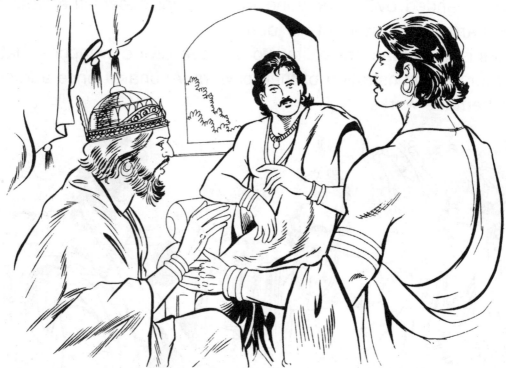

But it delighted Shakuni. He dashed to the chamber of Duryodhana who was sitting there with his friend Karna. Shakuni told them too how Draupadi and Pandavas were getting hell in the forests. It pleased Duryodhana and Karna.

Karna suggested to Duryodhana, "Friend Duryodhana! I think we should also go to the wilds to enjoy the nature. Watching Pandavas in trouble would give us added pleasure. What do you say?"

Duryodhana liked the idea, "Good thinking, friend. And what do you say, dear uncle?"

"Nephew! Karna said just what I was going to suggest."

After Shakuni's approval, Duryodhana got up and went to seek permission of Dhritrashtra. The King thought that his son had a change of heart and felt sympathy for his cousin brothers. So, he gladly gave permission hoping that they might patch up.

Since Arjuna's return, Pandavas had been living in Kamyak forest. The very next day, Karna, Shakuni, Duryodhana along with their wives and a large army stormed there. They camped at a distance from where Pandavas cottage and their activities could be easily seen. They spent some days in hunting. Then, Duryodhana wished to play water games with his wives in a lake situated not far away from Pandava's cottage. He ordered his soldiers to level the ground.

Incidentally the Gandharva King Chitrasen had already arrived there for a swim with his wives and his army. When the soldiers of Duryodhana reached there, the Gandharvas drove them away. The soldiers reported this to Duryodhana which enraged him. He set out with Karna and Shakuni to teach them a lesson. The army was with them.

Chitrasen was no push over. As soon as he saw Kaurava army, he launched a fierce attack. Kaurava army could not even properly take a stand. They fled. Chitrasen used his hypnotizer weapon at the fleeing army. All the soldiers got frozen in whatever position they were. Then Chitrasen turned his attention on Karna. He attacked Karna with such ferocity that Karna was frightened. When his chariot got smashed to pieces Karna ran for his life. It was a disgraceful act for a warrior. Even Duryodhana condemned the cowardly behaviour of Karna. After Karna, Chitresen pounced on Duryodhana. In no time Duryodhana and his wives were taken prisoner and marched to the camp of Chitrasen. Duryodhana was feeling miserable and cursed the betrayal by Karna. He didn't know what to do. His wives understood the gravity of the situation. To save themselves from further disgrace, they sent a secret messenger to Pandavas cottage to seek help from Yudhishthira. The messenger explained the situation and conveyed how badly his sisters-in-law need his help.

❏ ❏

PANDAVAS TO DURYODHANA'S RESCUE

When the messenger reached at the cottage of Pandavas the brothers were sitting outside preparing for a Yajna. The messenger revealed the situation. He said, "King! Your sisters-in-law have sent me to you for seeking your help. Please rescue them."

It made Bheema and Arjuna laugh. Bheema remarked, "It is a good news. Chitrasen has done what we wanted to do."

Yudhishthira didn't like it. He said with a mild displeasure, "Bheema! You shouldn't say or think that way. We shouldn't laught at Duryodhana's misery. After all he is our brother. We shouldn't tolerate any outsider harming any member of our family. Infact, we must teach a lesson to the person who has dared to dishonour our family."

The smiles vanished off the faces of Bheema and Arjuna. They picked up their arms and went straight to the place where Duryodhana and his wives were being held prisoners.

They started a fierce battle against Gandharva army and drove it away. It scared Chitrasena. He quickly loaded Duryodhana and his wives in his chariot and tried to fly off into the skies. But Arjuna used a divine weapon and brought down the chariot.

As soon as the chariot landed back, Bheema moved to it and off loaded Duryodhana and his wives. Chitrasena knew Arjuna well because he had taught him music at Amravati. He extended his hand of friendship to Arjuna. Arjuna readily accepted it and asked, "Friend Chitrasena! Why did you take Duryodhana and his wives prisoners? Kindly explain."

"Dear friend! I will explain in detail, listen..."

Gandharva King Chitrasen revealed how the arrogant and foolish Duryodhana was camping there with Karna and Shakuni merely to watch Pandavas and Draupadi suffering in the jungle to derive pleasure out of it and to make fun of them later on. When Lord Indra found out the evil intentions of Duryodhana, he got angry. So, he had sent him to

Kamyak forest to put Duryodhana in trouble and to give some harsh treatment. That was why Chitrasena had taken Duryodhana's wives prisoners. Chitrasena hoped that the humbling experience of being rescued by Arjuna and Bheema would in future make Duryodhana feel ashamed.

And Chitrasena added, "He would feel small whenever he faces you two. The power has gone to his head. Infact Duryodhana is mean by nature. He has cheated you on every step and in every deal. He is jealous of you. The way he tried to humiliate Yudhishthira and Draupadi in open court proves how lowly character he is. Yudhishthira sent you to help him out because he does not know the basic purpose of Duryodhana in coming to this forest. So, I wish to meet Yudhishthira to explain things to him. Then, he will do as he deems fit."

"Al right, friend. Come."

Then Chitrasena, Arjuna and Bheema trooped to Yudhishthira along with the prisoners. Gandharva King paid obeisance to Yudhishthira who got him seated beside him with due respect. Chitrasena narrated to Yudhishthira the evil intentions of Duryodhana. The revelation made Yudhishthira grave. He spoke, "O Gandharva King! I am grateful to you that you did not slay Duryodhana and his friends. Your kindness is praiseworthy. O King! I thank you for honouring me with your kind visit to my cottage. You have done your job and feel free to proceed to your heavenly abode."

Chitrasen departed leaving the rest back. Before final departure he freed the Kaurava soldiers from his hypnotic freeze spell.

After his departure, Yudhishthira said to Duryodhana, "You should not pay heed to the advice of evil friends. Such mistakes sometimes cost very dear and bring humiliation. That is all I will say. Return back to Hastinapur with your wives and friends. Be careful."

Duryodhana was too ashamed to say anything. He returned to his camp with his wife.

Duryodhana departed for his capital. Having been rescued by Pandavas was a matter of great shame. Getting killed at the hands of Chitrasena would have been better, he thought. And Duryodhana was feeling deep anger at Karna who had betrayed him in the battle.

JAIDRATHA PUNISHED

Pandavas peacefully lived at Kamyaka. One day, Jaidratha, the King of Sindhu happened to pass by Pandavas, cottage. Incidentally he was husband of the Kauravas sister, Dushala. He saw Draupadi who was standing by outside the cottage. Her beauty aroused Jaidratha. He stopped his chariot and sent a soldier to find out who the beauty was and why she lived in that desolate place. The soldier returned after talking to Draupadi and reported that the lady was Draupadi, the wife of mighty Pandavas. Her husbands were out on hunting. Being related to the family, Draupadi had invited him in.

Jaidratha drove his chariot to Pandavas cottage.

Draupadi greeted him, "Welcome, O King. I will bring water for you to refresh yourself. My husbands will come back from hunting shortly."

Jaidratha saw his opportunity in the absence of Pandavas. He tried to entice Draupadi, "Why do you suffer by living with Pandavas. Come with me and enjoy life as the queen of my heart."

"Rascal!" Draupadi felt outraged and she spoke in angry tone, "How dare you say such lowly thing! Can't you even honour our relationship? A woman of our family is your wife which makes me your sister. You have betrayed your low breeding. Don't you know that making Pandavas enemies means death?"

"Look darling! Anger does not suit beautiful women. My proposal is for your benefit. As far as Pandavas are concerned, I am not afraid of them. If they are warriors, so am I. Now if I go, you will think that I got scared of Pandavas. So, you must come with me."

He lunged at Draupadi.

Draupadi tried to evade him but he caught hold of her wrist and dragged her out to put her in his chariot. Draupadi struggled.

"You lowly creature! Let my hand off. You are inviting your death!" Draupadi screamed and called out to the priest Ayudhomya.

The scream's had already brought the priest out of his hut. He came to stand before Jaidratha's chariot and warned, "Jaidratha! Let Draupadi off. Or the anger of Pandavas will ruin you for your misdeed."

Jaidratha ignored him and drove away his chariot.

The chariot was followed by his soldiers and the priest Ayudhomya.

Meanwhile, when Pandavas returned from hunting, a maid told them about what had happened. Their eyebrows arched at the outrage. Pandavas ran and caught up with the soldiers of Jaidratha.

Yudhishthira saw the priest following the soldiers and he angrily said to Arjuna, "Look! Our family priest is after the soldiers. Destroy all the soldiers and then we will rescue Draupadi from the clutches of Jaidratha."

Arjuna challenged the soldiers and a battle began. The soldiers were no match for the might of Arjuna. In a short time many lay dead and rest ran away.

Pandavas got the priest on their chariot and it raced to get Jaidratha.

Up ahead, Jaidratha was driving his chariot and looking back for any chasers. He spotted Pandavas racing at him and realised the danger he was in. Jaidratha quickly dropped Draupadi down and himself drove on.

Pandavas raced to her.

She told Pandavas with great revulsion what Jaidratha was upto. Then she challenged, "If you are really warriors you shall punish Jaidratha right away. I will feel soiled until that villain is not slain."

Bheema was the angriest of all the Pandavas. He was just raring to go after Jaidratha. His intention was to smash Jaidratha's head with his mace into pulp and drag his body to dump at Draupadi's feet. Yudhishthira sensed Bheema's anger and tried to cool him down, "Brother Bheema! No doubt that Jaidratha has done most outragious act but don't forget that he is husband of our sister Dushala. Please cool down."

But Draupadi was hell bent on revenge and she rebuked Pandavas. Bheema and Arjuna ran to get Jaidratha.

Meanwhile, Jaidratha was relaxed because he thought that release of Draupadi would cool down Pandavas and they won't bother to come in his chase. He slowed down his chariot and looked back. No one was chasing him.

But suddenly he heard sounds of approaching horse hooves. Looking back, he could make out the huge figure of Bheema on a chariot. Arjuna was with him. It terrified him.

He raced his chariot but there was no escape from Pandava brothers. Their chariot streaked ahead to block the path. Bheema jumped down in ferocious mood and marched to Jaidratha who stood petrified. Huge hands of Bheema grabbed Jaidratha by his hair and banged him down like a toy.

"Lowly animal! You dare to put your dirty hands on our honour!" Two or three mighty whacks of Bheema turned Jaidratha half dead.

Bheema grumbled, "I am not killing you because our brother Yudhishthira does not want you dead for the sake of sister Dushala. Now Draupadi would decide your fate."

The brothers took Jaidratha to their cottage with his hands and feet bound by ropes like a pig. They untied him there.

Jaidratha fell on Yudhishthira's feet seeking mercy. He caught Draupadi's feet calling her 'sister' and begging for his life. Yudhishthira signalled to Draupadi to pardon him. Though she was very angry yet she decided to honour Yudhishthira's wish.

Draupadi said to Bheema, "I forgive him as your elder brother wishes. But his misdeed must be punished. So, release him after shaving his head to let everyone know of his disgrace."

Bheema loved to do that.

Before departing, the chastised Jaidratha touched the feet of Yudhishthira and Draupadi. But in his heart he vowed to settle the score some day.

❏ ❏

SHIVA'S BOON TO JAIDRATHA

Jaidratha didn't want to go to his kingdom with the disgrace of the shaven head. A desire to take revenge on Pandavas had started burning in his heart. He decided to do penance to earn the blessing of Lord Shiva. He did deep meditation on the bank of the river Ganga. His penance pleased Shiva and He appeared before him. He said, "Jaidratha! Your devotion has pleased me. I grant you a boon."

"O Lord", Jaidratha prayed, "If you are pleased, please bless me to be victorious over Pandavas."

"That is impossible...," the Lord spoke, "Pandavas are invincible and so shall they remain. I can only grant you a boon that on a certain day, you will be able to check the advance of four of the Pandavas." And Shiva disappeared. Jaidratha was sad. So much penance earned him tittle rewards. Only gain was that during that period his hair had grown.

He silently went to his capital.

❑ ❑

YAKSHA'S QUESTIONS FOR PANDAVAS

After Jaidratha episode, Pandavas left Kamyak forest and settled in Swait forest. Here, they spent most of their time in doing religious duties. One day, Yudishthira was sitting outside his cottage when a Brahmin came to him and said, "O valiant Pandava! Help me."

Yudhishthira rose up in respect and asked, "How can I be of service to you, Brahmin? You are welcome to our cottage and any help."

"A deer has taken away my churner and the churn. Please get me back those items which I need for yajna. I will be grateful to you."

"How did it happen?" Yudhishthira asked in surprise.

"O Pandava Gem! I had hung those two things by a tree branch. Suddnly, a deer came there and starting rubbing its body against the tree. Those two items fell down and got entangled in the horns of the deer. The deer ran away when I tried to take them off its horns. Kindly find that deer and retrieve those things." The Brahmin explained and pleaded.

All the five Pandavas set out in search of the deer. They ran around in the forest for hours without any success. The brothers got very tired, hungry and thirsty. Yudhishthira said to Nakula, "Brother! Will you climb up on a tree and survey around for some source of water?"

Nakula went up a tall tree and looked around. He informed, "Brother! I see a pond a little distance away." He got down and asked, "I will go to bring water if you permit me. Shall I? Meanwhile you can rest."

Yudhishthira agreed to it.

Nakula went Northwards and reached the pond. Before filling his pitcher with water, he decided to drink the water himself. As he extended his hand towards water, a harsh voice warned, "Stop! This pond is mine. If you want water you must answer my questions correctly. Then, you will be allowed to take the water."

Nakula ignored the voice and dipped his cupped hand in water. As soon as he did that he lost consciousness and rolled over.

Then, Bheema, Arjuna and Sahdeva came and met the same fate.

At last, Yudhishthira arrived there puzzled. He also heard the warning.

Yudhishthira asked, "Who are you? Kindly show up."

A Yaksha (human of a superior sacred breed) showed up. Yudhishthira paid obeisance to him and said, "O Respected Yaksha! You can ask. I'll try to answer."

"Who or what is man's greatest ally?" Yaksha questioned.

"Patience."

"What is more fickle then wind?"

"Mind."

"What is a man's greatest enemy?"

"Anger."

"Losing what makes one rich?"

"Greed."

"What is the greatest wonder of a man's life?"

"A man sees people dying everyday and finds no one who has ever survived death. But he refuses to believe that he would also die one day."

Yaksha, infact was Yamaraja himself in disguise. The answers of Yudhishthira greatly satisfied him. He spoke, "Your answers have pleased me. So, I have decided to revive one of your brothers. Tell me, which one?"

Yudhishthira folded his hands, "O King of Dharma! We five brothers are sons of mothers, Kunti and Madri. Out of Kunti's three sons, I happen to be alive. But mother Madri's both sons Nakula and Sahdeva lie dead here. I request you to revive one of them."

Yudhishthira's principled wish delighted Yamaraja. He said, "O Yudhishthira! I praise your noble sentiments. I am reviving all your brothers."

All the four Pandavas came back to life.

Yudhishthira was overjoyed to see his brothers back alive and in good health. He embraced and kissed the foreheads of his brothers one by one.

Yamaraja remarked, "Son! You are indeed great. You have conquered the weaknesses that even the greatest fail to defeat. You have indeed tamed hunger, lust, anger, greed, grief and arrogance. I am pleased. You shall be known as Dharamaraja from now on. You can ask for two boons. Ask anything."

"Lord! we have promised a Brahmin to get his churn and churner which had got entangled in the horns of a deer. The deer has disappeared. As the first boon, bless us to be successful in that mission. For the other boon bless us to successfully complete the thirteenth year of secret exile."

Now, Yamaraja transformed himself in his real form and spoke, "O Yudhishthira! I am no Yaksha but Yamaraja. That deer was also I. I put on that act to test you. Here, take the churner and the churn and give them to that Brahmin. As for the second boon I direct you to go to the capital of King Virata. Pass the year of secret exile in his service. You will stay safe and untraced there."

With these words Lord Yamaraja disappeared.

Pandavas returned to Draupadi. They handed over the two items to the Brahmin.

They discussed the 13th year of exile which was to be secret. The twelve years were about to end.

In accordance with the direction of Yamaraja, Pandavas decided that Yudhishthir would enter King Virata's court as an advisor Brahmin. Bheema would go there as a royal cook, Arjuna was cursed to be a eunuch for a year, so he could become music and dance teacher of the princess Uttara. Nakula would join royal stable as a syce, Sahdeva would work as supervisor of royal cow sheds and Draupadi would seek employment as the Queen's personal maid under the false name 'Sairandhri'.

And the six set out for the capital of King Virata.

❏ ❏

PANDAVAS IN SECRET EXILE

In Viratanagar, Pandavas went to the court separately in indivisual capacities and sought employment according to their stated qualifications. King Virata in consultation with his Prime Minister, gave them jobs as they appeared very competent persons. Draupadi as Sairandhri was sent to Queen Sudeshana.

Draupadi's beauty and trim figure pleased the queen. She asked, "You accept to be my private maid?"

"Yes, Honourable Queen. But on two conditions," Draupadi said and added, "I won't wash dirty dishes and I won't eat anyone's left overs."

The queen readily accepted the conditions.

Thus, Draupadi, was employed as the personal maid of the queen.

KEECHAKA EYES DRAUPADI

Keechaka was Queen Sudeshana's brother and the Chief commander of Virata's army.

Incidentally, King Virata was a weak King. He had little control over the administration. Keechaka was the real power and the indirect ruler. He was a great warrior.

One day, he came to the Queen's chamber to meet his sister. And his eyes fell on Draupadi. Her beauty cast a spell on him. Keechaka lusted for her. He made up his mind to get that maid become his bed mate.

That day he kept quiet.

But next day he cornered Draupadi and said, "O Beauty! You work here as a maid but don't look like one. You deserve to be a consort of a great warrior like me. Come to my palace, I will give you all the comforts and the riches of life. Perhaps you don't know that I am the real ruler of this kingdom. My wish is law here."

The proposal made Draupadi angry and she said, "You filthy worm! How dare you talk to me like that? Don't think that I am an ordinary maid. Remember, I am a Gandharva woman. My Gandarva men are always around to protect me. If they come to know of your evil intentions then, they won't spare you. You will find no place to hide."

Draupadi's rebuke made Keechaka run to his sister. He told her, "Sister! I have fallen for your new maid. I won't feel satisfied without getting her. Do something to send her in my arms."

"Brother! Sairandhri is my special personal maid. I can't force her to do anything. I may send her to your palace on some pretext. It will be upto you to lure her to accept your love. But remember, you won't force her in anyway."

Keechaka went away satisfied.

❑ ❑

KEECHAKA KILLED

A few days later, a festival fell. The Queen needed some items for a traditional worship. On his sister's advice, Keechaka bought those items and kept them in a chamber of his palace. On the eve of the festival, the Queen said to Draupadi, "Dear! I will perform Shiva worship tomorrow. My brother has bought some needed items for it and kept at his palace by oversight. Get me those items."

Draupadi didn't want to go to Keechaka's palace but she could not refuse the Queen's request. So, she went to Keechaka's palace and asked for the worship items. Keechaka's eyes twinkled to find Draupadi in his chamber. The sight of Draupadi made him lustful. He tried to grab

Draupadi but she was alert. She gave him a sharp push. Keechaka staggered back and Draupadi ran out of the chamber.

She dashed to the court of King Virata who was sitting with his ministes and courtiers. Keechaka also arrived there on her heels. He grabbed Draupadi in the presence of all of them. No one dared to stop him. He rained blows on Draupadi, kicked her, abused her and warned her of dire consequences. Then he went away.

Draupadi also left the court shortly after. Her body seethed in rage at the humiliation. She went straight to sleeping Bheema and woke him up. She told him what Keechaka had done to her. The outrage of Keechaka inflammed the fiery temper of Bheema. It looked that raging Bheema would go and tear Keechaka apart. But Draupadi had sobered up by then. She cooled down Bheema and advised him to use restraint. Then, they discussed the matter purposefully. Bheema got an idea. He suggested to Draupadi to play Keechaka's game and act attracted to him. Then, Draupadi was to lure him to the dance chamber at midnight for love session.

Draupadi agreed to play the game.

Keechaka was after Draupadi relentlessly. One day, Draupadi let Keechaka corner her and press her to surrender to his desire. She was waiting for such an opportunity. After some usual 'No-No' she smiled enticingly and whispered, "Alright, you win."

Keechaka almost squealed in delight. He asked Draupadi to slip into his bed chamber at night. Draupadi said, "I have told you that Gandharvas are alwasys around me. Going to some one's chamber can be dangerous. Meet me in dance chamber. I shall be there at midnight waiting for you."

Draupadi informed Bheema of the planned meeting.

Before midnight, Bheema went into the dance chamber in the guise of a woman and sat down.

Meanwhile, Keechaka killed time in drinking. When midnight came, he set out of his chamber to have fun with Draupadi.

Keechaka, in drunken state entered the dance chamber. He was pleased to see a figure wearing Sairandhri's dress. He was too drunk to notice the physical difference. With open arms, for a passionate embrace, he lurched forward. Bheema waited for him. As he came closer, Bheema picked him up of the floor and banged him down. Keechaka was confused. He forced his eyes open and saw angry face of Bheema staring down at him. Bheema was on his chest. Before Keechaka could gather his wits, Bheema's iron fist smashed his apple and broke the collar bone.

Keechaka shuddered to death without making a sound. Now, Bheema slipped out and went to his chamber.

In the morning, Keechaka was found murdered in the dance chamber.

The news of the murder of her brother brought queen Sudeshana running to the dance chamber. Her dead brother's terrified face shocked her. King Virata was stunned. He was worried that without Keechaka his kingdom was not safe.

The queen returned to her palace and summoned Sairandhri.

She asked her if she knew about the murderer. Sairandhri replied, "I don't know anything about it. I had warned your brother that my Gandharvas were always around to protect me and not to expect anything of me. But he ignored my warning and tried to harass, outrage and dishonour me. He even thrashed me in the court. May be, my Gandharvas have taken revenge. May be, not. Who knows?"

The queen looked frightened. She stammered, "So, it is also possible that your Gandharvas might some day try to harm us also. I request you to leave my service and seek employment elsewhere."

Draupadi stood still and silent. Then, she spoke, "As you order, O Queen. But I request you to grant me thirteen days to find a new job."

The queen could not displease Sairandhri for fear of the Gandharvas.

❏ ❏

DURYODHANA'S ILL ATTEMPTS

When the secret exile period of Pandavas began Duryodhana started his attempts to locate them to send them on a further 12 year exile. His spies had been scouting all over without success.

But Pandavas and Draupadi had vanished in thin air. All efforts to trace them failed. It greatly annoyed Duryodhana. The time was fast running out.

The news of the murder of Keechaka pleased Duryodhana. He had a wish to conquer Viratanagar and make it a part of Hastinapur. But he could not attack Viratanagar due to Keechaka. Keechaka's murder aroused suspicions in the mind of Duryodhana. The talk of Gandharvas was mystifying. He told his chieftans that he suspected the hand of Pandavas behind the murder of mighty Keechaka and that the maid Sairandhri had all the signs of being Draupadi.

Meanwhile, King Susharma of Trigarta Kingdom had come to Hastinapur. His kingdom bordered King Virata's, Matasya that had Viratanagar as its capital. Keechaka had made lot of trouble for Susharma. He suggested to Duryodhana, "Friend! This is the opportunity to take over Matasya kingdom. You attack it from the north and I will from the south. Without Keechaka the kingdom will fall without a battle. We shall share it half and half."

Karna also supported the idea. He said, "The suggestion is great. If we find Pandavas there, their secret exile will be blown up.

Duryodhana accepted the proposal. He asked Dushasana to make preparation for war, "Ready the army for the invasion of Matasya kingdom."

Then, he said to Susharma, "Friend! You carry out your part of the plan and invade Matasya from the south. We will follow up with attack from the north."

❏ ❏

MATASYA INVADED PANDAVAS EXPOSED

The very next day, Trigarta army launched an attack on Matasya kingdom from the south and captured a large part of land. The soldiers of Susharma took all milch cows and buffaloes in their possession.

From the north, Hastinapur armies invaded Matasya.

The citizens of Matasya were terror struck. All of them fled towards the capital, Viratanagar.

The spies brought the news of invasion into the palace. The King got frightened. He was not a courageous man and was incapable of defending against the enemies.

He consulted his adviser, Yudhishthira who was there under the name 'Kanka'.

Kanka assured the King there was nothing to worry about. He asked the King to prepare the army and took upon himself to lead the soldiers into the battle. He got Bheema, Nakula and Sahdeva also to join the battle.

The King accordingly readied his army for war.

The King and the Queen now looked composed. Kanka's talk had given them hope for some miracle from the new employees.

Yudhishthira and the three brothers led a part of the army and it ran into Kaurava army. A fierce battle began. The Kaurava army was shocked to see the skill and the bravery of Matasya army soldiers. It was told that the battle would be a cakewalk in absence of Keechaka. The battle raged on.

It continued till the sunset.

The battle stopped for the night and the warriors returned to their respective camps. Susharma dishonestly took King Virata prisoner after the end of the day's battle. Matasya soldiers were demoralised. A soldier ran to Yudhishthira to inform him of the deceit of Susharma. An angry Yudhishthira said to Bheema, "Brother! King Virata has been taken prisoner by deceit. He has to be freed."

"Don't worry. I will go after dishonest Susharma, "Bheema assured and addressed to Virata's soldiers, "Attention! No one shall retire to the camps until King Virata is not freed. Come!"

The soldiers moved under the leadership of Bheema. The battle again began in fading light. The soldiers of Virata fought aggressively. King Susharma's chariot broke down.

He jumped off his chariot. King Virata was with him as a prisoner in the same chariot. He too jumped down. The destruction of Susharma's chariot stunned his soldiers. King Virata took advantage of it and snatched the dagger of Susharma and tore his way though enemy soldiers to reach his army.

Susharma tried to run when he found Bheema confronting him. But it was no easy escaping Bheema's anger. He grabbed the King and threw him down. As Bheema raised his mace to smash the head of Susharma, Yudhishthira called out, "My brother! Don't kill the wretch. Spare his life."

Bheema pinned down Susharma with his knee and warned him not to look towards Matasya kingdom again. Bheema spared him when Shusharma promised the same.

Now, greatly encouraged King Virata stood by the side of Kanka alias Yudhishthira and challenged Duryodhana's army. They drove away them. King Virata had gained an incredible victory. He said, "Kanka! The credit of this victory really goes to you and my new employees whom you often call brothers. You are a warrior inspite of being a Brahmin. You are now the real power of my kingdom in place of Keechaka."

On the other side, the defeat of Susharma and Dushasana's army brought Karna into the battle field with his army. He advanced towards Virtanagar capturing Matasya lands and its properties and live stock.

The citizens ran to the palace of Virata and informed prince Uttar about the new challenge and their loss of the live stock.

The prince was childish and timid. He had already lost his chariot driver in the battle against Dushasana. Without his chariot driver he was reluctant to go to the battle. For him, it was like committing suicide.

Arjuna heard his talk and he asked Sairandhri to tell the prince that his sister's music teacher, Brihannalla (Arjuna's name as eunuch) was an expert chariot driver who had once upon a time served Arjuna.

Accordingly, Sairandhri told about the eunuch teacher and suggested that he take his services. Arjuna's name impressed the prince and he agreed.

So, they came into the battlefield. Karna was wreaking havoc.

Karna and the sight of his worriors scared the prince, Uttar. He had no conrage to face such mighty worriors. He wanted to go home. So, he pleaded with Brihannalla, "Chariot driver! Turn back the chariot and take me back to the palace. I can't face these fiery warriors."

"No prince. You should not go back without winning back your live stock and lands. The people will take you for a coward. The women of the palace and kingdom will laugh at you. Will you be able to take it?"

The prince had no answer.

"The true warriors don't run away from the battlefield. If you are getting frightened then take over the driver's seat. I shall fight the battle."

The prince at once agreed to do so.

Then, Arjuna drove the chariot to the place where he had hidden his divine weapons before the start of the secret exile period. Arjuna retrieved his favourite Gandiva bow and other weapons earned from Lord Shiva and the gods of Amravati. He drove back to the battlefield and put the prince in the driver's seat. He stood up on the back seat to wage the battle. He was still in eunuch dress but started shooting arrows on Karna's army.

Karna's soldiers laughed to see an eunuch in the battle.

But Dronacharya had his eyes fixed on the eunuch. He was watching his actions closely. And he recognised him as Arjuna. He leaned over of Bhishma and announced, "I think that eunuch is our

Pandava Arjuna. We must protect Duryodhana since we are fighting on his side."

Karna heard him and remarked, "So what if he is Arjuna? We are not afraid of him. Today we shall get him in battle..."

Duryodhana cut in, "Friend Karna! Don't lose cool over what Guru said. Imagine if he is really Arjuna, how nice it is going to be for us! Pandavas will again go into 12 year exile."

Arjuna was not upset at the laughter of Karna and his soldiers. The 13 year exile period of Pandavas had expired only a day ago. So, he had no reason to hide his identity. To formally announce his presence Arjuna blew his Devdutta conchshell.

The sound of Devdutta delighted Duryodhana. He jumped for joy and squealed, "That's him, Arjuna! Look at my luck, Karna! Pandavas go into exile again. Ha!"

"You are mistaken, Duryodhana," Grandman Bhishma corrected him, "Don't you even realise that their secret exile has also ended. Now only thing that remains is for you to decide whether you will give back their rights or fight a war against them."

"What rights, Grandman? We are the sole rulers of Hastinapur. I won't give them an inch of my land. We must better prepare for war."

"Alright. You go back with these milch cattle and half the army. I, Karna and Drona would hold Arjuna."

Duryodhana slipped away. But Arjuna noticed his absence from the battlefield. So, he asked the prince to race the chariot on the road leading to Hastinapur to get back the cattle.

Prince Uttar turned the chariot towards the road that led to Hastinapur. Karna blocked the path of Arjuna. A charged up Arjuna showered such fierce volleys of arrow that Karna fled from the battle. His arrows crippled Kaurava army.

Arjuna's charge was so stunning that Bhishma and Drona just watched helplessly. Then, Arjuna used his spell binder weapon and the enemy soldiers and warriors became frozen as and where they were. Taking advantage of it he went after Duryodhana and recaptured all the cattle after a hair raising battle.

Then, he left the cattle in the care of the prince and went off to hide his divine weapons. He reached the palace in his eunuch guise.

Meanwhile, with the help of mighty Bheema, King Virata had dealt a crushing defeat to King Susharma. He was given a hero's welcome by the citizens of the capital. He got worried when he didn't find Prince Uttar in the palace. He asked about him. Princess Uttara replied, "Father! He has gone to battle against Kauravas with Brihannalla as his chariot driver."

Before King Virata could react a soldier arrived to report, "Victory be to the King. The prince has driven away the Kaurava army and won back all the cattle."

The King was overjoyed. He rewarded the soldier with his pearl necklace and announced, "Decorate the city and the palaces to celebrate the historic victory of my valiant prince."

The citizens of Viratanagar started raising welcome arches along the path the prince was supposed to return by. The valiant deed of the prince had warmed the hearts of the people.

King Virata was a proud person and a happy man. He couldn't wait to welcome his hero son. To pass the waiting time he invited Kanka for a game of chess. The game began. The King crooned, "See! My brave son has defeated the so called mighty Hastinapur army!"

"That was natural, O King. After all Brihannalla had agreed to be his chariot driver," Kanka alias Yudhishthira remarked matter of factly.

King Virata didn't like the words of Yudhishthira. The expression of joy went off his face and he looked angry. He took a hard look at his advisor and growled, "You idiot! How do you compare an eunuch with my brave son? You speak as if without that miserable eunuch my son wouldn't have defeated Kauravas. What ugly idea! It is a occasion of joy. So I forgive you. If you ever again say such disrespectful words I will have your evil tongue cut off." King Virata threw pieces of chess at Yudhishthira's face when he showed no signs of regret.

His face bled at many places. By chance Sairandhri saw it. She ran to him and began wiping blood with the corner of her saree.

A soldeir came to announce arrival of the prince.

"Bring him in at once." The King said excitedly. He was too eager to hug his son and congratulate him for his historic deed.

But the prince had come in on his own. He touched the feet of his father. Then, he saw Yudhishthira's bloodied face. He asked in shock, "How did you get hurt, O Sir?"

"I punished him, son. The fool was camparing you with that eunuch teacher. Imagine!"

"Father! You hit him inspite of knowing that he was a Brahmin? You must apologize to him. And you don't know who he really is."

"Really is? Who is he, son?"

"Father! He is the eldest Pandava, Yudhishthira. He was passing his secret exile period here as a Brahmin advisor, Kanka."

It stunned King Virata.

Then, the prince revealed the entire story. Virata was very sorry for his act and felt very small. With folded hands he said to Yudhishthira, "O Great One! I am very sad for my ignorant behaviour. I seek your pardon. It is my good fortune that you chose my capital to pass your period of difficulty. And you protected us from the invaders. O great Pandava! I will feel honoured if you kindly accept the hand of my daughter, Uttara for your younger brother Arjuna."

"How is that possible, O King? My brother Arjuna has served as teacher of your daughter. For a teacher, a student is like a son or a daughter. If you are so keen on alliance between our families, we can accept the daughter Uttara as bride of Arjuna's son, Abhimanyu." Yudhishthira suggested.

King Virata liked the proposal very much. He at once announced the engagement of Uttara to Abhimanyu.

Abhimanyu was summoned to Viratanagar.

Pandavas also invited King Drupada, his son Dhrishtadhyumana, Lord Krishna and Balrama to the marriage.

On due date, Abhimanyu and Uttara were married according to the customs and traditions with great pomp and show.

❏ ❏

WHY MAHABHARATA WAR?

Pandavas had fulfilled both the exile conditions imposed on them as a result of losing in the gamble. Now the natural thing for Duryodhana was to return the kingdom of Indraprastha to Pandavas and live peacefully. But evil minded Duryodhana was not ready to concede even an inch of the land.

Through the efforts of Krishna and King Drupada, a meeting of Kings was called at Viratanagar with a view to making Duryodhana return the Pandavas' kingdom to them. Krishna delivered the opening address to the assembled Kings, "Honourable sirs! As you are all well aware that Duryodhana cheated Pandavas of their kingdom in a gamble with the help of Shakuni who rolled loaded dice. Earlier through similar deceit he tried to disgrace queen Draupadi in their court. And the lac-house conspiracy to destroy Pandavas in no more a secret. On numerous other occasions Duryodhana tried to harass Pandavas in many ugly ways. Inspite of all this Pandavas honestly fulfilled the terms of exile. Now Pandavas must get back their kingdom. All the members present here know the position of Duryodhana. He does not want to give the kingdom of Indraprastha back to Pandavas. Now he is talking of hereditary issue. He claims that he is the legal heir of King Vichitravirya. He is using strange arguements to prove that point. He says Pandu, the father of Pandavas was made a temporary King because of the blindness of his father Dhritrashtra, who was born blind and was destined to stay blind forever. So, Pandu was no temporary King as he claims. We must get together to get justice for Pandavas."

Panchala King Drupada rose to say, "Honourable guests! Krishna has put all the facts before us. Krishna stands for justice. He is always on the side of the truth. We must uphold the truth by getting Pandavas their kingdom back to them."

Now, Balrama rose to speak. He said, "I don't agree with my brother

Krishna and King Drupada. To me the claim of Duryodhana looks justified. He is indeed true heir to King Vichitravirya's throne. Pandu was given the crown to serve as working King because elder brother Dhritrashtra was blind. It was Dhritrashtra's kindness that he gave half the Kingdom to Yudhishthira for the sake of the peace in the family. But Yudhishthira could not hold on to his share of kingdom. Duryodhana has every right to keep the kingdom gambled away by Pandavas. It is a different matter if the elder Pandava, Yudhishthira himself goes to Duryodhana and begs for Indraprastha and he gives back the kingdom out of pity."

Infact, Balrama had never forgiven Pandavas for Arjuna's act of kidnap of his sister, Subhadra and the marriage.

Balrama's views enraged Yadava warrior Satyiki. He got and spoke harshly, "I am amazed at what Balrama has said. How does he consider use of loaded dice and dishonesty correct thing? If Duryodhana was so keen on the game of dice why didn't he ever invite Yudhishthira for a match before the partition of Hastinapur kingdom. The gamble was a consipracy to take away kingdom from Pandavas. Dice was rolled by well known trickster Shakuni. The simple minded Pandavas got cheated. It must be remembered that Pandavas didn't lose their kingdom. They only lost a bet for which they had to fulfil two exile conditions. The conditions have been fulfilled and Pandavas must get back their kingdom."

After a lot of debate, overwhelming majority reached at a decision that Pandavas had right claim to their kingdom. It was worked out that a proper messenger would go to Hastinapur on behalf of Pandavas and request King Dhritrashtra to make his son see reason and return Indraprastha to Pandavas. It was also decided that Pandavas and their allies must prepare for war to fight for justice if the peaceful means failed.

King Drupada's family priest, Sanjay was chosen to go to Kauravas court as the representative of Pandavas.

❏ ❏

SANJAY IN KAURAVAS COURT

Sanjay presented the case of Pandavas in the court of King Dhritrashtra. Grandman Bhishma agreed with Sanjay. He rebuked Duryodhana, "Son! You know that Pandavas are invincible. Still they have sent a representative to settle the issue peacefully. You must accept the peace offer and do justice to them. Don't be adamant. Pandavas are not the ones who would sit quietly. They will wage a war to win back their throne. Then you will lose your part of kingdom too."

Dhritrashtra too was of the opinion that forcing Pandavas to war will be suicidal. Bheema gave him shivers. He would see Bheema in his dreams tearing open the chest of Dushasana and smashing the thigh of Duryodhana. Seeing him thinking on the lines of Bhishma angered Duryodhana. He said, "Father! Don't worry about our fate. If Pandavas are great warriors our side also is no pushover. No Pandava can match our Grandman Bhishma in the battle. And you know well that Grandman is bound by his vow to defend and obey the wishes of Hastinapur crown. And Guru Drona is also on our side being a servant of Hastinapur court. Arjuna is merely his student. My friend Karna alone would take care of him." He declared his final intention, "I will not spare even a needle point size of land for Pandavas. And I will defend my kingdom till my last breath."

The declaration of Duryodhana brought a pin drop silence in the court. Bhishma and Dhritrashtra looked pained. Dhritrashtra suggested that Duryodhana atleast seek the advice of Krishna who had a fair mind. But Duryodhana rejected the suggestion on the plea that Krishna was partial to Pandavas. When Duryodhana displayed his uncompromising mood, an anguished Gandhari lamented, "Why did I have to bear a pig headed son like you who would listen to no one's sincere advice! You will repent and bring ruin to our family."

Duryodhana ignored her lament. Saddened Dhritrashtra and Gandhari left the court in a huff.

❏ ❏

SANJAY RETURNS

Pandava camp was discussing the matter. Yudhishthira was ready to settle for anything for the sake of peace. He even said that he would be satisfied with only five villages spared by Duryodhana if it avoided war.

Meanwhile, Duryodhana had made up his mind not to spare even a needle-head size of land to Pandavas. Infact, Duryodhana was certain that without any base or resources Pandavas won't be able to wage a war. How many kings would actually support them against Hastinapur's might?

Sanjay came back from Kauravas court and reported whatever had happened at Hastinapur. The sum total of his report wat that the mission had failed.

A pained Yudhishthira said to Krishna, "Dear Krishna! I don't understand what I should do in this situation. Please show me way."

"I want to go to Duryodhana to try to put some sense into him and to warn him not to invite disaster," Krishna spoke.

Inspite of Yudhishthira's fears for his safety, Krishna went to Hastinapur to make one last attempt to ward off bloodshed. He argued and reasoned with Duryodhana. He asked him to spare only five villages to satisfy Pandavas. Duryodhana refused to budge. Then he met Kunti and returned with a message from her for Yudhishthira.

The message was a hint for war. She had told to Krishna—"Krishna! Tell Yudhishthira to think gravely keeping the justice in mind. No one must be meted out injustice and no one should give up one's just right. If peace moves fail then don't hesitate to fight for your right. My blessings are always with them. Assure Draupadi that her humiliation shall be duly avenged."

Yudhishthira became grim upon hearing the message.

❏ ❏

KUNTI MEETS KARNA

Kunti had sent the message to her sons advocating war. But her mind was troubled about war. The worry was the valour of Bhishma, Drona and Karna. Her sons were brave but would they be able to tackle so many a great warriors?

She was assured about Bhishma and Drona that the two would not kill any of her sons. They loved them. But Karna could be dangerous.

So, she made a plan to meet him and try to win him over.

One morning, she reached the pond bank where Karna used to come to worship every morning. Karna gave her due respect but he refused to part ways with Duryodhana.

Kunti revealed to Karna that Pandavas were his real brothers.

Karna said, "You call me your son. So, I promise you that you will remain the mother of five sons as before. My death or Arjuna's won't matter."

Kunti returned disappointed.

☐ ☐

DHRISHTADHYUMANA IS PANDAVAS COMMANDER

Pandavas were in the meeting. All their warriors were present. Yudhishthira conveyed to them the intentions of Duryodhana. Then, he turned to his brothers and said, "There is no hope for any compromise or peace. So we must organise our army and workout strategies."

The Pandava army was divided into five units. Each unit was to be led by seven unit commanders. They included Drupada, Virata, Dhrishtadhyumana, Shikhandi, Chekitan, Satyaki and Bheema.

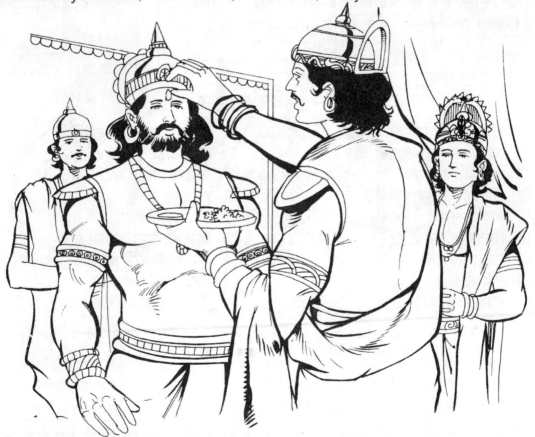

Dhrishtadhyumana was unanimously elected Chief Commander of the entire force. And he was ceremoniously installed in that capacity.

BHISHMA IS KAURAVAS COMMANDER

Meanwhile, Kauravas were also planning their strategies in the court. They had decided to make Grandman Bhishma as the Chief Commander of Kaurava army. He was the most experienced soldier on their side. On two conditions, Bhishma had agreed to carry that responsibility. He had made it clear to Duryodhana, "For me the sons of Dhritrashtra and Pandu are equally dear. But due to my vow to defend the crown of Hastinapur, I shall be fighting the war on your side. But I won't kill any of Pandava brothers, only their soldiers. The second condition is that as long as I am Chief Commander of your army, Karna would stay away from the battlefield. I know that he is very dear to you. But he has always opposed me and my suggestions."

When Karna learnt about the conditions of Bhishma, he said, "Friend Duryodhana! As long as Grandman Bhishma is the Chief Commander I won't also fight as a warrior."

That solved Duryodhana's problem ironically.

ARJUNA OPTS FOR KRISHNA

The preparations for Mahabharata war were in full swing. The ally kings were marching towards the battlefield of Kurukshetra with their armies to join the respective sides. The Yadava chieftans of Dwarika were famed warriors. Krishna was their supermo. So, both Kauravas and Pandavas wanted them on their respective sides.

Krishna greatly favoured Pandavas who were his close relatives and friends. But Duryodhana too wanted him on his side as he too was related to him. He took the initiative and reached Dwarika first. Krishna was asleep in his chamber after having his mid-day meals when Duryodhana entered. Arjuna foliowed him moments later. He found Duryodhana already seated on a chair on the head side of the bed of Krishna. Arjuna sat down near Krishna's feet and waited for Krishna to awaken.

After awhile, Krishna awoke and saw Arjuna sitting infront of him.

He couldn't see Duryodhana as he was a little behind his back. He sensed his presence when Arjuna and Duryodhana greeted him simultaneously. Krishna greeted them both and asked for the purpose of their visit. Bot sought his support in war.

It was a bit of a problem for Krishna. He could not turn away any of them. So, he called his brother Balrama for consultations of decide his response.

Balrama arrived there in no time. When Krishna explained the situation to him, he looked confused and in two minds. It was a tricky problem for him too. He chose the middle way to play safe. He asked Krishna to stay neutral. Krishna didn't like that idea. Then, Balrama left the matter for Krishna to decide. And to clear his confusion he set out on a pilgrimage.

After Balrama's departure, Duryodhana said, "Brother! I know that Pandavas are your favourites. But I hope that you will play fair and won't turn me back empty handed. I reached here first. So, I have the right to put my demand first."

Krishna spoke, "Prince! It's true that you came here first. But when I woke up I saw Arjuna first as he was sitting in front of me. Only later I realised your presence on the high seat behind me. I love Pandavas, no doubt. But I have equal love for you which you don't realise. But don't worry. I will disappoint none of you."

Krishna's talk pleased Duryodhana.

Then, Krishna addressed to both of them, "Listen carefully to what I say, friends. Being younger one, Arjuna will have right to the first choice. You must know about my army. We Yadavas are dauntless worriors. My army is made of famed warriors who have several victories to their credit. My army will go to one side and I to the other side. And I have taken a vow not to take up arms to fight in your war. Think over it. Arjuna! Tell me, do you choose me or my army?"

Arjuna at once said, "I choose you. I don't need your army. It makes no difference to me whether you fight or not."

Krishna smiled and accepted Arjuna option.

Meanwhile, Arjuna's demand had pleased Duryodhana. He chuckled at the crass stupidity of Arjuna.

Krishna granted his army to Duryodhana.

Duryodhana was so elated as if he had already won the war. Back in Hastinapur, he gave the exiting news of having Yadava army on their side to Shakuni and Karna. They were also very pleased.

After Duryodhana's departure, Krishna asked, "Arjuna! Why did you opt for me?"

Arjuna replied, "Lord Krishna! I want to defeat Kauravas. It was impossible without your wisdom and guidance. So, I naturally wanted you."

❑ ❑

DURYODHANA TRICKS SHALYA

The King of Madra, Shalya, the brother of Madri, who was the mother of Nakula and Sahdeva started with his army with great spirit to help Pandavas. He was a famed warrior.

Duryodhana had been trying to win over as many Kings as possible to his side by fair or foul means. He heard about the arrival of Shalya. In consultation with Karna and Shakuni he appointed a large number of his men on King Shalya's route. They gave great reception to Shalya everywhere and took great care of the comforts of the King and his army. Shalya was under the impression that those men had been deployed by Pandavas to make his journey smooth. Shalya prepared to reward the men. When Duryodhana learnt about it he presented himself to Shalya and disclosed that the men who served were his people and the arrangements were his efforts.

It shocked Shalya. He realised that cunning Duryodhana had tricked him. He was in a fix. How could he fight against his very nephews? But he was now in a moral bind. Sadly he asked, "Say, what can I do for you?"

"Uncle! I just wish one thing of you. Please fight on my side in this battle."

Shalya was benumbed. He was bound by courtesy to accept Duryodhana's request because he had unwittingly used the hospitality offered by Kauravas. He gave word to Duryodhana and went to meet Pandavas.

He met Yudhishthira and told him about his mistake. Elder Pandava said, "No hard feelings, uncle. You must honour your word. Our love and respect for you will remain the same. Duryodhana is a trickster. No surprise that he cheated you. We just need your blessings."

❑ ❑

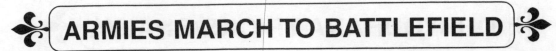

ARMIES MARCH TO BATTLEFIELD

After the preparations, Pandava army set out for the battlefield. Sounds of conchshells and trumpet calls of elephants rant the air.

Meanwhile, Kaurava army too marched towards Kurukshetra. It was made of thousands of chariot mounted warriors, war elephants, cavalry soldiers and hundreds of thousands of infantry men.

At Kurukshetra, on the two sides of a large area for battle, the armies pitched tents or made sheds. Duryodhana sent Shakuni's son, Ulook to Yudhishthira to announce that his army under the command of Grandman Bhishma had arrived to battle with Pandava army.

After consultations with Krishna, brothers, commanders and the Chief Commander Dhrishtadhyumana, Yudhishthira declared war.

❑❑

THE MAHABHARATA BEGINS

At appointed time, the armies faced each other in the battlefield of Kurukshetra.

Arjuna was on his chariot with Krishna as its driver.

Arjuna saw Grandman Bhishma, Guru Drona, his son Ashwatthama, Shalya and other relatives standing in the enemy lines. The thought of killing all those near and dear ones chilled him. Sentiments crushed his heart. He tossed aside his Gandiva bow and spoke to Krishana, "O Lord Krishna! How can I slay all those respected elders, friends and dear ones? For kingdom! shall I not go to hell? Or won't life become a living hell with blood of all those people on my hands? I don't feel like...any fighting. I won't."

The anguish of Arjuna didn't come as surprise to Krishna. He advised, "O Arjuna! A man must do his duty without any considerations to consequences because it is the very purpose of existence. Don't let worldly emotions cloud your mind. Everything and everyone in this cosmos is a fragment of God. So, you do nothing. Whatever happens is merely God in action. Pick up your bow and fight to fulfil your role." The advice given to Arjuna by Lord Krishna in detail is known as 'Geeta' which became the moral and spiritual treasure of human race.

Krishna's revelation brought Arjuna back into the world of hard facts and harsh truths. He suddenly became so keyed up to the battle that he picked up his bow and raised a battle cry, "Warriors! Rain death on the enemy!"

He blew his Devdutta conchshell to declare war. His warriors also blew their shells creating frightening sound.

The sudden boil stunned everyone.

Then, suddenly Yudhishthira took off his armour and put weapons down in his chariot. He got off the chariot and walked towards where Bhishma's chariot stood. Arjuna and Krishna ran after him in confusion about what he was doing.

Bheema feared that peace loving Yudhishthira might put off the war.

Unmindful of what others were thinking, Yudhishthira went to Grandman Bhishma and said with folded hands, "Respected Grandman! We have been forced to wage a war against you. So, I have come to seek your permission to start the war and I pray for your blessings for the victory."

After getting the permission and the blessings of Bhishma, he went the Guru Dronacharya and Shalya to receive their blessings also. As soon as Yudhishthira returned to his side, the war began.

The leading column of Kaurava army was being commanded by Dushasana. Bheema was leading Pandava column.

Bhishma launched such fierce attack on Pandava army that the soldiers fell back. This angered Abhimanyu who dashed to the front and rained arrows on Bhishma and his warriors. The Kaurava warriors tried to surround him but failed.

Abhimanyu cut down Bhishma's chariot flag. By now, Pandava warriors had advanced to help him. They formed a security ring around young Abhimanyu and forced Bhishma to retreat.

Other warriors ware also fighting on different fronts. Virata prince Uttar was on his elephant. He attacked Shalya with ferocity and crippled the horses of the chariot of his apponent. It enraged King Shalya who threw a spear that went through the chest of Uttar. The prince died. But his faithful elephant ran at Shalya and wounded him badly.

The death of Uttar brought his angry brother Shweta in front of Bhishma to fight revengefully. They battled for several hours. Shweta also lost his life after he had put hundreds of enemies to death.

Thus, in the first day's war Pandavas suffered heavy losses.

The battle of that day sobered up Pandavas and their Chief Commander. They woke up to realities.

❏ ❏

THE SECOND DAY OF WAR

The next day, Commander Dhrishtadhyumana and Arjuna set their soldiers in planned formations and gave them pep talk.

Meanwhile, Duryodhana was happy with the result of the war of the first day. In great spiritis he encouraged his warriors, "Brave Ones! Our victory is certain. The first day's encounter has sent the enemy back licking its wounds. So, battle on to defeat the enemy."

Duryodhana's speech so enthused Kaurava warriors that they pounced on Pandava soldiers with a mighty charge. Pandava formations broke down and they suffered heavy casualties. their soldiers got demoralised.

Arjuna had to do something to revive their spirits. He asked Krishna to take him to face Bhishma. Bhishma rained arrows when he saw Arjuna's chariot coming at him. Arjuna cut down his arrows and pushed into Kaurava formations to wreak havoc.

It shocked Duryodhana. He said to Bhishma, "Grandman! Please checkmate Arjuna to stop the massacre." Bhishma tried to do that. But Krishna was driving the chariot so expertly that Arjuna looked like a fleeting shadow dealing death to Kaurava warriors. Duryodhana perspired. Bhishma's inability to tackle Arjuna made him wish for the presence of his friend Karna.

Meanwhile, Bheema too was havoc.

No Kaurava warrior could stand before him. He was moving like a one man juggernaut. Suddenly Duryodhana come across Bheema. One mighty blow of Bheema's mace sent down Duryodhana out of his senses. His driver cleverly raced the chariot out of the battlefield.

On the other side, warrior Satyaki rushed to Arjuna's help and he killed Bhishma's driver. The horses of the chariot went out of control.

Meanwhile, Dhrishtaadhhyumana was challenging Drona. He had taken a vow to kill Drona to avenge the insult meted out to his father, Drupada. They battled grimly. Drona was trying to handle the Panchala prince but the Panchala prince, the Chief Commander of Pandava army was proving too hot. He was too excited. He attacked Drona with his mace. When Drona blocked his every mace blow, he ran at him holding his dagger. Drona decided to attack instead of defending. He rained arrows and succeeded in wounding Dhrishtadhyumana. Bheema rushed to his aid. Bheema's mace blow stunned Drona.

When Duryodhana saw Drona under pressure against Bheema, he sent Karna's army to defend him. But Bheema beat the army back killing a large number of its soldiers. Kaurava army was at the receiving end. Grandman Bhishma had to rush to defend Drona against Bheema. To counter him Satyaki and Abhimanyu came to stand by Bheema.

Just then sun set and the end of the day's war was sounded.

❑❑

THE THIRD DAY OF WAR

On the third day, Bhishma planned a new army formations. The lead formation was to be led by Duryodhana. The complex formations gave Kauravas hope that Pandavas will fail to breach their lines.

The Pandava army was in semi-circular formation. One end was guided by Arjuna and the other by Bheema.

The sound of a conchshell started the war. It soon reached the peak of intensity and ferocity which surprised the warriors of both sides. More surprising thing was that inspite of fierce attempts no side could break through the other's line.

Shakuni arrived with his large army from Gandhar. But Satyaki and Abhimanyu blocked it and did not allow it to join the Kaurava army.

Then, Bheema invoked his son Gatotakacha who was born to demoness Hidimba. He materialised at once. The demon size Gatotakacha played havoc with Kaurava army. All the formations broke down and all hell broke loose. Even Bhishma and Drona looked shocked and terrified.

Bheema was battling with Duryodhana. Bheema blows sent Duryodhana to sleep again.

Again, his driver took the chariot out of the battlefield. He knew that if news of Duryodhana's passing out spread, the Kaurava soldiers would get demoralised. But it proved more damaging. The soldiers thought that Duryodhana had fled. Hence, they fell back.

And Pandava soldiers charged and massacred them.

Meanwhile, when Duryodhana regained consciousness he learnt about the massacre and the retreat of his army. Duryodhana ranted and cursed. He blamed Bhishma and Drona for having soft corner for Pandavas. He accused them of not putting their hearts in the war. Bhishma smiled and calmly said, "Son! I had already warned you that Pandavas were invincible. You won't listen to me. I repeat again that Pandavas will win only because their cause is just."

Duryodhana went away cursing everyone.

❑ ❑

THE FOURTH DAY OF WAR

Kaurava Commander Bhishma ordered the regrouping of his army. Pandava army was in high spirits and in full blood. It openly counter attacked. Soldiers and warriors clashed. To demoralise Arjuna, Duryodhana had hatched a plan. According to it Kauravas tried to corner Abhimanyu and kill him. Abhimanyu bravely fought back. Pandava commander Dhrishtadhyumana noted it and rushed to the defence of Abhimanyu. Both groups clashed. Bheema also ran in to protect Abhimanyu. Duryodhana set a group of rogue elephants at Bheema who drove them away. After all he had the power of thousand elephants. Duryodhana came to challenge him accompanied by a dozen of his brothers. Bheema was in such rage that he smashed eight of his brothers to death and deal Duryodhana a crippling blow. The wounded Duryodhana launched a secret weapon at Bheema which rendered him senseless.

This brought Gatotakacha there roaring in anger. He drove away Kaurava soldiers.

Commander Bhishma and Drona had no answer to him. The battle contineud till sunset. The war claimed thousands of soldiers and hundreds of warriors on both sides.

❑ ❑

WAR INTO FIFTH DAY

Pandava army was feeling high because the fourth day had belonged to them, on the whole. On this day, Kaurava army was trying a still new formation to foil the attempts of Pandavas to break in. Pandava army was moving under the leadership of Bheema. Shikhandi, Satyaki and Dhrishtadhyumana were closely behind him. The war began, Bhishma shot fierce volleys of arrows. But Arjuna was shadowing him. He neutralised the volleys.

Drona too was proving ineffective. Kaurava soldiers were dying.

It drove Duryodhana mad. He made Drona the target of his criticism. Drona said, "Duryodhana! You don't know the depth of Pandava's power." And he made fierce attacks on the enemy. Satyaki and Bheema came forward to take him on and checked him. Bhishma and Shalya came to bail out Drona. As Bhishma prepared to attack, Shikhandi the eunuch came to face him. Bhishma withdrew from the battlefield announcing that he wouldn't fight a eunuch.

The war raged on till mid-day. Thousands perished.

In the afternoon, Duryodhana sent Bhurishrava against Satyaki who had slain thousands of Kaurava warriors so far. No one had been able to tame him. Bhurishrava was a famed swordeer. He too had slain scores of opponents. He was proving too good for Satyaki who fell wounded. At this, his ten sons came to take on Bhurishrava. The swordeer cut down all the ten of them. Bheema saw this and he took Satyaki away from battlefield in his chariot.

Meanwhile, Arjuna was taking a heavy toll of Kaurava soldiers.

As Arjuna's arrows would claim Kaurava soldiers the Pandava soldiers would raise victory cries.

The sunset arrived and that ended the fifth day's war.

❏ ❏

SIXTH DAY'S WAR

For the sixth day, Pandava army stood in 'Crab' formation. Kaurava army was in 'Bird' formation.

The sixth day's war was barbaric. In the very begnning, Drona's driver got killed. He attacked Pandava army with vengeance. Pandavas gave befitting reply. But the army formations broke up and it became free for all as soldiers fought indivisual battles.

Duryodhana yet again ran into Bheema who badly injured him. He saw his soldiers panic. It pained him. After the end of the day's battle, he barged into Bhishma's tent and complained about it.

Bhishma consoled him and said, "Do not have nay suspecion about the soldiers, Duryodhana. Our soldiers are very loyal. They are fighting for the victory. Have no doubts."

The royal physician applied medicines to Duryodhana's wounds.

❏ ❏

THE SEVENTH DAY

For the seventh day, Bhishma adopted a new strategy. Duryodhana was feeling healthy after the night's rest.

Yudhishthira too had set up his army in an impressive and unique formation. The battle had to be fought on many fronts.

Arjuna had run into Bhishma. The bitter opponents Drupada and Drona were engaged in a duel. Shikhandi was battling against Ashwatthama. Satyaki was up against a demon named Alambush who was on the Kaurava side, and Pandava's man-demon Gatotakacha was tackling old warrior King Bhagmal.

The duels were fierce. Ashwatthama defeated Shikhandi. King Bhagmal got better of Gatotakacha. Drona drove away king Drupada and killed his son Shankha. Satyaki beat back Alambush.

The battles raged on.

Yudhishthira was taking on Shatayu. He killed Shatayu's driver and forced him to flee. Kaurava priest Kripacharya was engaged in a battle against Chekitan. Meanwhile, Dhrishtaketu had wounded Bhurishrava but he was a warrior of different kind. Even in wounded state he beat back Dhrishtaketu.

On the other front, Abhimanyu had beaten the daylights out of the brothers of Duryodhana. He let them off alive because he remembered that his uncle Bheema had taken a vow to get the blood of one of them, Dushasana for washing the hair of Draupadi.

He preferred to challenge Bhishma. Pandava brothers rushed to Abhimanyu's side when they saw Bhishma preparing to hit back.

Just then the war for the day came to an end as the sun set.

❏ ❏

WAR INTO 8TH DAY

Bhishma set his army in 'Turtle' formation for the war of 8th day. Dhrishtadhyumana countered it by positioning his army for three pronged attack to be led by Bheema, Satyaki and Yudhishthira.

Bheema's eyes were always on the look out for the brothers of Duryodhana. He had already claimed eight of them. The Kaurava demon Alambush had killed Eravan, the son of Arjuna, born out of Uloopi of Naga country. It greatly irritated Gatotakacha. Eravan's dead

body made him roar in anger and go on a Kaurava killing spree. Kauravas soldiers ran for their lives. Duryodhana had to rush in to stop the rampaging son of Bheema. Gatotakacha threw a secrte weapon at Duryodhana. Duryodhana escaped but his elephant got killed.

Duryodhana's heart skipped a few beats. It was a lucky escape. Drona's soldiers ran to help Duryodhana. Gatotakacha's war cry brought Bheema to him to give support. The fierce battle raged on resulting in heavy loss of life on both sides.

Then, the day's war ended.

❑ ❑

THE NINETH DAY

The nineth day's battle was as fierce as the war of the earlier days. So far Kauravas had suffered more losses. So, Duryodhana spoke to his brother, "Dushasan! we must fight with greater push. And we must not allow Shikhandi to confront Grandman Bhishma. He does not fight against eunuches due to a vow he has taken. Pandavas might take

advantage of it. So we should be very careful and vigilant." And Duryodhana went to challenge advancing Pandava army.

❏ ❏

TENTH DAY'S WAR
BHISHMA PUT OUT OF ACTION

Before going in to the tenth day's war, Arjuna took a vow that he would put Grandman Bhishma out of action on that day. So, eunuch Shikhandi was riding the chariot along side Arjuna. Shikhandi was avowed to be the cause of Bhishma's death.

Arjuna started raining arrows on Bhishma standing behind Shikhandi.

Arrows tore through Bhishma's chest. He frowned for a moment, then smiled. He knew that his end had come. He took in more arrows but did not hit back.

His vow was not to fight against a eunuch. It must be remembered that Shikhandi was incarnation of Amba, the daughter of King of Kashi whom Bhishma had forcibly brought for Vichitravirya along with her two sisters. On Amba's request she was allowed to go to Shalva King whom she loved. But he refused to accept her because he thought that Bhishma had defiled her. Amba committed suicide taking a vow to take birth to cause Bhishma's death because of whose act her life had been ruined.

With his body full of arrows Bhishma got off his chariot and lurched towards Arjuna's chariot with a sword in his hand to seek out Arjuna who was behind Shikhandi. But Arjuna was alert. His arrows cut down Bhishma's sword and shield.

Bhishma staggered and fell down to get propped up by the arrows that protruded out of his back, He looked like a man lying on the bed of arrows.

It stunned and shocked everyone.

Then, all the warriors raced towards him to see the greatest of the warriors and to pay tributes.

Arjuna and Krishna also ran to him forgetting all about the war. Bhishma's head was hanging down which was putting him in great pain. Arjuna was tearful.

Bhishma said, "Son! Give my head a support."

Duryodhana barked to his soldiers to at once fetch soft pillows. Bhishma shook his head and nodded to Arjuna. Arjuna shot three arrows in the earth below Bhishma's head to serve as arrow head rest. Grandman blessed Arjuna. He declared that he would release his soul when the sun would be northerly. He said to Arjuna, "I feel thirsty. Get me water."

Arjuna shot an arrow in the ground and a fountain of water came out to fall into Bhishma's mouth. He again blessed Arjuna and said to Duryodhana, "Duryodhana Son! There is still time. Change your heart and thinking. Don't let my sacrifice go to waste. At my cost make peace with Pandavas, or Kauravas will perish."

Arrogant Duryodhana went away feeling cheated.

When Karna learnt about Grandman Bhishma's fate he came running to the spot. He wept clutching the feet of Bhishma and said sobbing, "Grandman! Don't leave us please. You always despised me because I was from a lowly weaver family. I worshipped you. How I wish I were born to a high family to earn your love!"

"Karna, my son! come to me," Bhishma called to him and put his hand lovingly on Karna's head and whispered, "Son! you are no son of weaver. Kunti is your mother, I know. You are as dear to me as Pandavas. Dear Karna! I didn't despise you because you came from weaver family apparanty. I was angry with you because you let yourself become a part of the evil plans of Duryodhana. You could have easily stayed away from his schemings. Your support was making him more and more arrogant and unreasonable. Only you could have reformed Duryodhana had you wished. But you didn't. Anyway, you still can do it. This war can end with my end."

Karna pleaded very politely, "Respected Grandman! I know Pandavas are my brothers. But I am too weiged down by commitments to Duryodhana to be able to act on my own. I am too indebted to him. I can't betray him in whatever he wishes to do even if it means fighting against my own brothers. I am also in a moral bind. Kindly bless me to be successful in fulfilling my duties to a friend."

Bhishma heaved a long sigh and remarked, "Well, do what you like, son. Fate is against us. This is the end of the road for me. Pandavas are fighting for a just cause. So, they shall win. Remember that."

Meanwhile, Duryodhana was looking for a new Chief Commander for his army. Bhishma suggested, "Karna! You have won many battles. You must take over the command of Kaurava army to defend Duryodhana. My best wishes are with you."

After that Karna mounted his chariot and departed.

❑ ❑

DRONA IS NEW COMMANDER

Duryodhana was overjoyed to see his friend Karna coming to the battlefield in his chariot. He knew that in Karna Kauravas had an able commander. Accordingly Duryodhana asked him to take over as Chief Commander of his army. But Karna had a suggestion which Duryodhana could not reject. Karna said, "Friend! There are a number of warriors in our army who deserve to be chief commander. They are fully qualified. But giving one this job might make others jealous. So we must look for an elderly person who should be acceptable to all. Such a person on our side is Guru Dronacharya. I will suggest his name."

All others agreed on Guru Drona's name. He was duly installed as the new Chief Commander of the forces of Kauravas.

All the warriors of Kauravas side welcomed the new Commander. Drona set Kaurava army in 'Cart' formation. All the Kauravas hoped for the victory against Pandavas under Drona's leadership.

WAR INTO 11-12TH DAYS

The 11th day of the war was Drona's first day as Kaurava Commander. He faced the same irony as the previous commander Bhishma did. Both had a soft corner in their hearts for Pandava brothers but were fighting on the side of Kauravas. Their hearts would not allow them to physically harm any of the Pandavas. Duryodhana and Karna knew about it. So, they always suspected the commitment of the two to the war and thought of ways to test them. Duryodhana said to Drona to test him, "Guru! If you do a task for us we shall be grateful. Get us Yudhishthira alive."

Drona agreed because it didn't mean any physical harm to Yudhishthira. He did not know the aim Duryodhana had in his mind.

Meanwhile, Pandavas learnt about it through an informer. So, Pandava Commander decided to defend Yudhishthira at all costs.

In the battle, Drona tore through Pandava formations to reach Dhrishtadhyumana.

Sahdeva and Shakuni fought a mace battle nearby. Nakula was beating back uncle Shalya. On one side, Bheema was on the rampage with his mace. His mace was driving away Kaurava soldiers.

The eleventh day was one of the grimmest of the war. The soldiers and warriors were engaged in do or die battles. Both sides suffered heavy loss of life.

Pandava warriors Satyaki, King Virata and Abhimanyu were wreaking havoc. Abhimanyu was particularly in fiery mood. He was battling with four warriors, Paurava, Jaidratha, Kritvarma and Shalya. When Bheema saw it he rushed to help his nephew.

Drona was sorry to see the four mighty worriors fail to contain young Abhimanyu who now had his mighty uncle Bheema by his side. Bheema's mace blow felled Shalya. His death dealing mace frightened the Kaurava soldier who ran away in all directions. Drona was looking for Yudhishthira. When he spotted him, Drona raced his chariot towards his target. Yudhishthira was alert.

He rained arrows at Drona. But Drona reached to him braving the arrows. Some Pandava soldiers screamed that Yudhishthira had been caught. It brought Arjuna to the spot. He rained arrows with such ferocity that Drona had to withdraw empty handed.

Drona had failed and he had realised that as long as Arjuna was there he could not succeed in capturing Yudhishthira. He suggested to Duryodhana, "Son! As long as Arjuna is there, getting Yudhishthira would be impossible. Do something to draw away Arjuna."

The King of Trigarta, Susharma volunteered to take Arjuna away from that part of the battlefield. He regrouped his warriors and made them take a vow that they won't leave the battle till Arjuna was not dead.

They were given special armour and dress to prepare for a suicide mission. Death or success was their aim.

Then, Susharma challenged Arjnua for a battle. Arjuna always accepted a challenge. It was a matter of honour for him. He gave the responsibility of the defence of Yudhishthira to Dhrishtadhyumana and prepared to take on Susharma and his brigade of warriors.

Krishna turned the chariot towards Susharma and his warriors. Arjuna shot deadly arrows at the challengers and began to put them to death. Susharma and his soldiers counter attacked bravely. Arjuna was so engaged in the battle with Susharma brigade that Drona got the chance to send his soldiers towards Yudhishthira.

Dhrishtadhyumana stood between Yudhishthira and Drona's soldiers.

Drona knew that he was fated to die at the hands of Dhrishtadhyumana. So, he turned away towards King Drupada. He drove away Drupada's soldiers in no time and made to sudden dash towards Yudhishthira from otherside. But Dhrishtadhyumana was very alert. He swifty moved to stand between Drona and his target—Yudhishthira. The battle raged on. In this clash, Pandava army suffered heavy loss but saved Yudhishthira. Dhrishtadhyumana lost his two brothers and a son of Virata. When Bheema learnt about this bloody clash he ran to the spot accompanied by Satyaki, Shikhandi, Nakula, Virata and Drupada.

This greatly strengthened security ring around Yudhishthira frustrated Drona. Duryodhana and Karna came to his help along with a group of elephants. But It did not work. Bheema beat back elephants who ran trampling upon Kaurava soldiers.

The great warrior Bhugdutta was also fighting nearby. When he saw elephants crushing Kaurava soldiers, he mounted his famed elephant Supratika and ran at Bheema. The elephant was trained for battle. In one lunge it reached Bheema, got him by its trunk and banged him down on the ground.

Pandava warriors feared for Bheema's life. But Bheema had a rock like tough body. He rolled over to get underneath Supratika. Bheema had great knowledge of the anatomy of elephants. He speared the soft parts of the underbelly to cause such agony that the elephant ran away from the battlefield with Bhugdutta on its back.

Meanwhile, Arjuna was dealing with Susharma's warriors. The most of them had been killed. The few who still survived were fighting on.

Arjuna's mind was worried about the safety of Yudhishthira.

As loud groans of Supratika reached to Arjuna from that direction he feared for the worst. He asked Krishna to drive the chariot to Yudhishthira. Krishna did so. When Susharma and his surviving warriors saw Arjuna's chariot racing away they ran after it raising the cries of victory. They thought that they had scared away Arjuna. Arjuna was too concerned about the safety of Yudhishthira.

In this confusion, King Susharma was able to launch two divine weapons aimed at Arjuna and Krishna each. This drove Arjuna mad with anger. He shot three arrows to cut down the incoming missiles. Then, he gave one to Susharma to beat him back.

Krishna drove their chariot to the place where Bheema was engaged in a battle with Bhugdutta who had managed to return to the battlefield after calming down his elephant.

Arjuna's return enthused the Pandava soldiers. They fought with renewed vigour.

Arjuna shot arrows at Bhugdutta. The elephant's protective armour got smashed to bits. It made the elephant groan in pain.

Bhugdutta himself got pierced down by arrows.

The old King Bhugdutta and his elephant both feel down dead.

Two of the Shakuni's brothers named Vrishaka and Achala came forward to take on Arjuna. In no time they went downwards felled by the deadly arrows of Arjuna. Maddened Shakuni pounced on Arjuna but he too got badly injured. He fled from the battle ground.

❏ ❏

THIRTEENTH DAY'S WAR

The previous two days had proved costly for Kauravas. And Drona had failed in his mission to capture Yudhishthira. He was consulting something with his warriors when Duryodhana barged in the tent of Drona. He was in great anger and spoke rudely to Drona who did not like the tone of the language of Duryodhana. He remarked dryly, "Duryodhana! Don't consider the enemy weak and foolish. Arjuna is very cleverly protecting Yudhishthira."

In the battle, this day too, Susharma and his remaining warriors challenged Arjuna. Arjuna's chariot again ran after Susharma brigade. Drona siezed the opportunity and tried to get Yudhishthira. He launched a fierce attack on Yudhishthira and his army. Though a number of stalwart warriors were defending Yudhishthira yet Drona's thrust was so powerful that Satyaki, Bheema, Kuntibhoja and Virata were unable to contain it. All worried about the safety of Yudhishthira.

Then, Abhimanyu arrived there.

ABHIMANYU IN TRAP

This day, Drona was leading his army in circle-within-circle formation called 'Chakravyuha'. It was a very complex formation. Only Arjuna, on Pandava side knew to breach that formation. And Abhimanyu also knew but only to breach in. Once Arjuna was telling about Chakravyuha to Subhadra. Abimanyu was then in his mother's womb. He heard the method to breach in. As Subhadra feel asleep, Arjuna stopped the narration mid way. Thus, Abhimanyu could not learn how to breach out of it. He asked his chariot to be driven to Drona. He wanted Bheema to follow him to force their way out of Chakravyuha after breaching in.

Abhimanyu's driver was reluctant to take such a grave risk. He spoke, "Prince! Being your driver it is my duty to give suggestions some times. Is it wise to breach in complex Kaurava formation like Chakravyuha? It is dangerous. Drona is an experienced warrior and war planner. Your knowledge about it is only half baked."

Abhimanyu laughed and remarked, "Dear Sumittara! Your suggestion is wise. I am happy you care about me so much. But I am the nephew of Krishna and the son of Arjuna. This is no time for fears and doubts. Please drive the chariot to Dron".

The driver raced the chariot.

The Kaurava army was puzzled to find Abhimanyu's chariot racing towards it. He was a terror striking and expert archer as his father Arjuna. Abhimanyu was running in raining arrows. The soldiers panicked. The outer ring of the formation broke up. It worried Duryodhana. He advanced to take on the young warrior. Abhimanyu tried to capture Duryodhana alive. Drona sent a contigent of warriors to protect Duryodhana. They saved Duryodhana in the nick of the time before Abhimanyu could grab him in a daring attempt.

Duryodhana felt humiliated. The bravery and audacity of Abhimanyu rattled him. So far, only Bheema and Arjuna were his bugbears. Now Abhimanyu too had scored against him. It was a matter of shame for him. Simply not tolerable for arrogant person like him. Duryodhana made up his mind to destroy Abhimanyu by hook or by crook, even by violating the basic rules of war.

Drona too was feeling jealous at the dare devilry of the young warrior. So, he approved Duryodhana's evil plan. As a result, Drona, Kripacharya, Shalya, Karna, Shakuni, Ashwatthama and Jaidratha came together to lay a seige to Abhimanyu who battled on regardless.

He killed a king named Ashmakh, pierced the armour of Karna and sent Shalya to sleep with a sharp arrow. When Shalya's brother attacked, Abhimanyu felled him with just one arrow.

Now Karna faced Abhimanyu. But even before he could string his bow, Abhimanyu cut the bow down. A warrior who ran in to help bowless Karna got killed.

The defeats Abhimanyu was dealing out was further humiliating Kauravas. Their pride was being trampled upon. All around Abhimanyu were long worried faces of Kaurava warriors. It made Jaidratha launch an attack on Abhimanyu with his band of warriors who were fresh and spirited. It encouraged others who made a ring around the young warrior. Bheema who was to follow Abhimanyu was held outside this ring.

Thus, Abhimanyu got cut off and was isolated.

Jaidratha was outside this ring trying to block Pandavas. He remembered in time the Shiva's boon that he would be able to checkmate four of the Pandva brothers. He invoked Shiva and prayed that this was when he would like the boon to work.

It worked and Jaidratha was able to hold all the four Pandavas outside the ring in which Abhimanyu was trapped.

How could Shiva's boon fail?

Inside the ring, Abhimanyu was battling with seven warriors. And he was successfully beating them and not letting them gain the upper hand. No Kaurava warrior was able to stand up to him. Kaurava warriors were getting slain. This situation was worrying Duryodhana who was at a loss to know what to do.

The worried face of Duryodhana pained his son, Laxmana. He moved forward with his soldiers and challenged Abhimanyu. But he was no match to the Pandava prince. An Abhimanyu arrow claimed him which went through his heart. He fell down to die with a groan.

The agonishing death of Laxmana shocked Kaurava warriors. Duryodhana was grief stricken mad. He screamed, "Get this son of Arjuna killed. He is alone here like a cornered rat. Kill him! Don't worry about rules. Just slay him! He killed my favourite son."

Guru Drona, the Chief Commander of Kaurava army made no attempt to uphold the codes of war. He just nodded his sanction.

Six or seven warriors attacked Abhimanyu at a time.

Karna attacked from behind and smashed Abhimanyu's armour, bow, quiver and shield. It was the lowest point of Mahabharata war.

The young warrior did not surrender. He picked up a wheel of his chariot and attacked Kaurava warriors and killed many of them. Then, the wheel broke apart and the son of Dushasana dealt a mace blow to Abhimanyu who stayed on his feet. The brave youngman snatched the enemy's mace but didn't attack as the rival was now unarmed. But someone hit him from behind with mace and he fell down. A shudder and Abhimanyu's body lay still.

The death of Abhimanyu sent a wave of joy through Kaurava army. Pandava camp was grief stricken. Yudhishtira was the saddest person. He wept in his tent. He was at a loss to understand how would he explain it all to Arjuna and Subhadra. And how to console them?

The sage Vyasa arrived there.

Yudhishthira controlled his grief and prepared to welcome the sage.

Vyasa knew everything. So he consoled Yudhishthira, "Son! You should not grieve over the honourable death of a warrior."

Meanwhile, Arjuna was returning after disposing off the warriors of Susharma. He was feeling some bad Vibes. He didn't know why. He got the answer to why when he reached his camp and learnt about the killing of Abhimanyu by deceitful means. He wept for his son.

Krishna tried to console him. Arjuna wanted to know how and who killed Abhimanyu. Yudhishthira informed him how Abhimanyu was trapped and the Pandavas were not allowed to enter the ring by Jaidratha. Yudhishthira revealed that according to the information Abhimanyu had been killed in gross violation of the rules of the war.

Arjuna could well imagine how tricky Kauravas might have slain his son. Arjuna passed out in grief. When he came back, he was angry and craved for avenging the death of Abhimanyu. He took a vow that he would slay Jaidratha before the sunset the next day.

❏ ❏

THE FOURTEENTH DAY

On the very morning of the fourteenth day, the information reached the Kaurava camp that Arjuna had taken a vow to slay Jaidratha before sunset on that day. It chilled Jaidratha. He went to Duryodhana to express his wish to return to his capital for security reasons. Duryodhana would not agree. He assured that all arrangements had been made for the security of Jaidratha. He need not worry, Duryodhana claimed. But Jaidratha was doubtful. He went to Guru Drona to express his fears. Drona also mentioned that his security was no problem and there was no need for any fears.

That day's Kaurava army formation was just for one purpose, defending Jaidratha. He and his army stood in the centre and other armies were posted all around them making several defence rings. It would be no easy even for Arjuna to get to Jaidratha. Dushasana came with a large army. Duryodhana stationed him in front of Pandavas to serve as the first defence wall. Dushasana challenged Arjuna. In acceptance of the challenge Arjuna blew his conchshell and the battle began. Arjuna drove away Dushasana and his army in quick time. Then he asked Krishna to take him to Drona. In front of Drona, Arjuna didn't launch any attack. He said, "Guru! I am after Jaidratha's blood. Tell me where he is hiding so that I fulfil my vow."

"Arjuna! His security is my responsibility." Guru Drona said and added, "You won't get to him without defeating me."

Arjuna put an arrow to his bow but before he could shoot Krishna advised that he shouldn't waste his time there. Krishna drove the chariot towards the left flank of the Kaurava army.

Kaurava warriors tried to hold Arjuna but they could not stand their ground when Arjuna began his onslaught. Some of them died. Others ran for their lives. Thus Arjuna broke through the outer defence walls of Kaurava army and reached the inner circle where Jaidratha hid behind several security rings.

The advance of Arjuna towards Jaidratha worried Duryodhana. He ran his chariot to Drona and informed him of the Arjuna's push. Drona gave Duryodhana a divine chest shield and asked him to engage Arjuna in the battle. Drona wanted to keep Arjuna engaged there and meanwhile he could try to take Yudhishthira prisoner.

Duryodhana, in that shield went to challenge Arjuna.

Watching Duryodhana coming at them Krishna alerted Arjuna, "Look! Duryodhana is coming to challenge you. This is the chance to finish off that evil character. Don't miss it."

Arjuna rained arrows at Duryodhana. But the divine chest shield blocked all the arrows. Arjuna took a close look at Duryodhana and realised that he was wearing some divine armour or shield. Without losing time Arjuna shot some invoked divine arrows. The horses of Duryodhana's chariot got killed and the wheels got smashed. Duryodhana too got hurt. Now he ran off the battle leaving Jaidratha to his fate. Saving his own life looked more important to him.

Meanwhile, Dhrishtadhyumana had engaged Drona to keep him away from Arjuna's mission of slaying Jaidratha.

The war was raging on. Because of the death of Abhimanyu Pandava warriors were battling with vengeance. The Kauravas army was under pressure.

Bheema was on rampage. His mace was smashing enemy heads all around. He had given a good beating to Karna and had killed several of the brothers of Duryodhana. Karna came back again to check Beema. But he got another hammering from Bheema. Karna's helplessness against murderous Bheema had stunned Duryodhana.

Then, Vikarna came infront of Bheema. He could not escape the rage of Bheema. His dead body brought tears to the eyes of Bheema. Because among a hundred Kauravas he was the only one who was truthful and justice loving.

Karna once more returned to face Bheema. On this day, Bheema had smashed 18 of Karna's bows.

Karna decided to fight a do or die battle. He rained arrows at Bheema with a new resolve. Bheema again broke his bow. It angered Karna and he shot such fierce volleys of arrows that he smashed Bheema's chariot and bow. Bheema ran at Karna with his sword and shield. Karna managed to save himself by skin of the teeth. He shot arrows at Bheema taking cover of his flag pole and broke his sword and shield. Bheema was now unarmed but Karna did not stop shooting arrows. He knew that if Bheema grabbed him, then he would beat him to pulp with bare hands. He could have killed Bheema but Karna had given a word to Kunti that he would only kill Arjuna or get killed. Lord Krishna saw Karna attacking an unarmed Bheema. He pointed it out to Arjuna. Arjuna's blood boiled at the cowardly act of Karna. He rained arrows on Karna with such speed and ferocity that Karna had to flee from the battle. Arjuna saw Satyaki engaged in battle with Bhurisharava. Bhurishrava was a great warrior. The presence of Satyaki there gave Arjuna cause for more worry for the safety or Yudhishthira.

Satyaki and Bhurisharva were wrestling after battling in archery and dagger fight. They were like too clashing mountains. Neither of them was yeilding to the other.

Krishna's clever eyes noticed that Satyaki was very tired and Bhurishrava was fresh. He hinted to Arjuna to help Satyaki. Arjuna thought over it.

Meanwhile, Bhurishrava had raised Satyaki up above his head and was about to slaughter him with a dagger. Arjuna shot his arrow and it cut off the dagger holding hand of Bhurishrava. Bhurishrava objected to it and sat down holding his severed hand. Arjuna reasoned, "A tired and unarmed enemy must not be attacked with weapon like you were about to do."

Suddenly, Satyaki got up and murdered Bhurishrava with his own dagger after snatching it from the severe hand. Everyone condemned Satyaki for his act.

Arjuna was looking for Jaidratha.

The time was running out. Sunset was only a short time away. Arjuna had not been able to kill him as avowed. Duryodhana said to Karna, "Friend! this day is very important. We must protect Jaidratha at all costs. If Arjuna fails to kill him before sunset he would kill himself out of shame. That will mean the end of half of the power of Pandavas. So defending Jaidratha means victory in war for us." Karna was too tired to fight any more. The battles with Bheema had sapped his energy.

Inspite of being at war since morning Arjuna was not looking tired. He was breaking through ring after ring of protective lines and nearing Jaidratha. He smashed through the last ring and killed Jaidratha's body guards. Now he faced Jaidratha. Their battle began. Both looked at the sun every now and then. The sun was kissing the horizon. Suddenly it became dark and Kaurava ranks jumped with joy.

Failure to fulfil vow saddened Arjuna. He was stunned and demoralised. Just then Krishna told him that the sun had not set. The darkness was an illusion created by him to make Kauravas drop their guard. He asked Arjuna to kill Jaidratha with an arrow that should fly his head to fall into the lap of Jaidratha's father who was doing penance for the safety of his son.

Arjuna wasted no time. He shot the arrow. The head of Jaidratha fell into his father's lap.

Krishna lifted his illusion and the sun shone again.

Kauravas were too angry to notice it. They thought that Jaidratha had been killed against all rules. It became a free for all war. The warriors were violating rules freely.

Pandava soldiers raised cries of victory at the death of Jaidratha. The sounds of conchshells rant the air. But Kauravas refused to stop war even after sunset.

Both sides lit up torches and the war raged on. Bheema's son, Gatotakacha stormed into Kaurava army with his terrifying weapons. He created hell for his enemies. The terror of Gatotakacha frightened Duryodhana. He asked his friend Karna to finish off the demonic son of Bheema at any cost. Karna knew the power of Bheema's son who had harassed him before also. Karna's heart sank. He was tired and weary of Gatotakacha. But he could not let down his friend Duryodhana. So, he came to face mighty enemy. Gatotakacha rained arrows on Karna. Karna knew that ordinary arrows won't impress the half demon Gatotakacha. Only some great divine weapon could deal with him. He had only one such weapon booned to him by Lord Indra which he had carefully spared so far to kill Arjuna. To save Kaurava army from utter destruction he used that weapon.

Gatotakacha fell down dead.

The death of the mighty Gatotakacha didn't end the war. Drona continued the fighting. Failure to protect Jaidratha had made him extremely bitter and hostile. He wanted to achieve some kind of victory as a consolation. He was fighting like a wounded lion and Pandavas were suffering heavily.

Krishna realised that at that rate Drona would destroy Pandava army. He proposed a trick to kill Drona. He explained the trick to Pandavas.

Krishna said, "Fan the rumours that Ashwatthama is dead. The news of the death of his son will shock him. He will throw down his weapons in grief and would sit down to mourn. That's when Dhrishtadhyumana must slay him."

At first, all rejected the suggestion as too macabre and deceitful. But Krishna argued and narrated how Drona had himself violated rules and played deceit to kill young Abhimanyu. Then others agreed.

According to the plan, Bheema killed an elephant called Ashwatthama.

Pandava soldiers made a loud noise screaming "Ashwatthama is dead! Ashwatthama is dead!!"

Drona was stunned.

He stopped shooting arrows. He wanted to confirm the news. But who would tell him the truth in the battle field?

He thought of Yudhishthira who never told untruth. He got his chariot driven to Yudhishthira and asked him to tell the truth.

Yudhishthira replied, "Yes, Ashwatthama is dead...an elephant of that name. Not your son."

But at Krishna's signal the soldiers made such a great noise with drumbeats, tomtoms, cymbals, blowing of conchshells that Drona could only hear 'Yes Ashwathama is dead....'

The rest of the sentence was drowned in noises.

Drona threw down his weapons and sat in his chariot grieving. Dhrishtadhyumana who always stalked him climbed into Drona's chariot and beheaded him with his sword.

It was a traumatic blow to Kauravas. The death of the Chief Commander brought an end to the 14th day of the war.

Kauravas had lost three of their greatest warriors Drona, Bhurishrava and Jaidratha.

❑ ❑

THE FIFTEENTH DAY

For the 15th day, Kaurava army had a new Commander—Karna. Shalya was appointed his chariot guide.

The auspicious hour for Arjuna-Karna confrontation was worked out by Pandavas with the help of astrologers.

The drum sounded for the beginning of the battle. Arjuna launched fierce attack on Karna. Bheema was by his side to lend support along with expert warriors.

Dushasana came with his army to support Karna. He rained arrows on Bheema.

The very sight of Dushasana filled Bheema with a feeling of great hatred. His blood boiled. In a rage he roared and pounced on Dushasana. Bheema dragged his enemy out of his chariot and threw him down on the ground with crushing force. To the horror of others Bheema smashed Dushasana's head with his mace and crushed every bone of his body. Then, he tore open dying Dushasana's chest and drank his blood. He collected some blood in an earthen pot for Draupadi to wash her hair with. Bheema, looking like a picture of horror, roared a challenge to Duryodhana. This day, Bheema struck terror even among Pandava warriors who watched his act frozen in terror.

King Shalya tried to buck up Karna. Blood curdling murder of Dushasana by Bheema had demoralised him. At last, Karna gathered his wits and started to battle Arjuna. He rained arrows at his foe with vengeance.

The news of the macabre death of Dushasana had broken the heart of Duryodhana. Ashwatthama consoled him and suggested peace pact with Pandavas. The suggestion enraged him. In great anger he collected his army and launched a fierce attack on Pandava army.

Meanwhile, Karna and Arjuna were battling, Karna was not within himself. He shot an arrow that rained fire. Krishna feared for Arjuna. In a flash he drove chariot in such a way as to lower the front portion by a foot and the arrow sailed overhead taking away Arjuna's had gear.

In reply angry Arjuna shot shower after shower of arrows.

Unfortunately the left wheel of Karna's chariot got stuck in a pot hole. It worried Karna. He called out to Arjuna, "Wait Arjuna! Let me pull the wheel out of the hole."

Before Arjuna could reply Krishna said, "Fine Karna! Did you object when Draupadi was outraged in court? Did you oppose the plan to burn Pandavas in the lac-house? Did you rebuke your friend Duryodhana when he poisoned Bheema? Did you remember rules when you murdered Abhimanyu in violation of all rules? Don't you feel ashamed in expecting us to give you the benefit of rules of war?"

Karna had no answer.

He gave up his effort of pulling out the wheel and got up on his chariot to shoot a powerful arrow. Arjuna's chariot shuddered when the arrow hit it. Karna got down again to pull out the wheel but failed. He tried to remember his guru's advice but he could not recall due to a curse put him by his guru.

Krishna gave Arjuna a signal to finish Karna. Arjuna was ready. He shot such an arrow that cut Karna's head off the body.

The death of Karna sent Duryodhana into deep mourning. He was incosolable. The frustration pain and grief stunned his mind. He could not think what he should do. So, he went to the family priest Kripacharya and poured to him his woes. Kripacharya consoled him and said, "Look son! This war has claimed most of your near and dear ones. What for? It got us nothing. Make peace with Pandavas."

Duryodhana shook his head angrily and spoke, "After the death of all those people how can I ask for any pact? What honour there is in it for me? How shall I show my face to my people? Shall I ever be able to live with myself? My conscience will always rebuke me."

Guru Kripacharya agreed with Duryodhana.

❏❏

WAR INTO SIXTEEN'TH DAY

On the 16th day of war, Kaurava army was led by king Shalya, ironically the maternal uncle of Pandavas. Among all the Kaurava warriors he was the only survivor who could command the army. He was valiant and crafty warrior, besides being famed archer, swordeer and mace welder.

Pandava soldiers were standing with their heads up and high. As Kaurava warriors kept dying one after another the morale of Pandava soldiers kept rising higher and higher. Pandavas launched attack on Shalya and the war hotted up.

A little while before sunset Shalya and Yudhishthira fought a dagger duel. Yudhishthira got a nice opening and in a flash his dagger claimed the life of King Shalya.

After his death, the surviving brothers of Duryodhana surrounded Bheema and rained arrows at him. It made no impression on Bheema who depended on his mighty mace. One by one Bheema blugeoned the Kauravas to death. And challenged Duryodhana to battle.

The fire of revenge still raged within the heart of Bheema as fiercely as it raged on the day Draupadi was outraged in the court of Kauravas. The insults heaped on Yudhishthira and Draupadi on that day were calling to him to take revenge by smashing the thigh of Duryodhana.

Meanwhile, on another front, Shakuni and Nakula were battling against each other. Shakuni was not only an expert in hatching conspiracies but he was a good warrior as well.

And he did not hesitate to use foul means to win battles. He was just thinking of some way to get the better of Nakula when Sahdeva arrived there. He threw a challenge to Shakuni, "O Devil's disciple! Your life is a bagful of sins. This war is the result of your misdeeds. You caused the destruction of Kauravas. Today I will despatch the bag to the hell."

Sahdeva shot a special arrow at Shakuni which went into his adam's apple and his head fell down cut off.

The last of Kaurava warriors was dead.

A soldier informed Duryodhana about the death of Shakuni. Duryodhana was petrified. He could think of no one who could now lead the Kaurava army. There was no one left to fight for him. Duryodhana lost all hope. His courage seeped off. He picked up his mace and walked towards the pond. He sat down on the bank of pond and brooded. He remembered the words of Vidura. Duryodhana thought, "Prime Minister Vidura was not wrong. He wanted me to reform myself. Buy I didn't pay heed to him. Ah! Now everything is finished. No use crying over spilt milk. I must pay for my deeds. There is no escape."

❏ ❏

SEVENTEEN'TH DAY'S WAR

On 17th day, Pandavas reached the battle field. There were dead bodies all around. But Kaurava army was nowhere to be seen. And Duryodhana had vanished.

Pandavas searched for him. They learnt that he was hiding in a pond. Pandavas went to the pond and challenged Duryodhana to come out. The challenge aroused his ego and arrogance. He came out with his mace growling like a beast. He asked Pandavas to battle with him one by one.

The arrogant challenge of Duryodhana was intolerable for Bheema.

He came forward for a mace duel. Duryodhana too was a good mace wielder. They fought a mace duel for quite some time. Pandavas were in high spirits because of the victory. But Duryodhana was demoralised and was fighting a losing battle. So, he was tiring out fast.

When Krishna caught the eye of Bheema he pointed at the thigh to remind him of his vow to break Duryodhana's thigh. The reminder gave Bheema revenge fever and aroused his anger.

In great rage he swung his mace and smashed the thigh of Duryodhana who fell down on the ground. Then, Bheema kicked his arch enemy's head several times. All prepared to depart leaving dying Duryodhana behind.

Suddenly Balrama arrived there having returned from his pilgrimage. When he learnt that Bheema had smashed the thigh of Duryodhana he flew into rage.

He barked at Bheema hatefully, "Fie on you, Bheema! Why did you hit below waist? It is against the laws of battle." He ran at Bheema to attack.

Krishna swiftly jumped to stand between Bheema and Balrama. He tried to cool down his brother, "Don't get so excited, big brother. Think of the wrongs he did to Pandavas and Draupadi. He took away their kingdom through tricks of Shakuni's loaded dice. He tried to disrobe Draupadi in public and make her sit on his thigh. So, Bheema took a vow to smash that thigh. He has merely fulfilled his vow."

But it didn't satisfy Balrama. He went away cursing Pandavas. Dying Duryodhana cursed Krishna. He said that Krishna was instrumental in misguiding Pandavas in doing wrong and unlawful things. He called Krishna a cunning schemer. He said many more unpleasant things to him. In the end he declared, "Krishna! I am dying. Dying in the battle like a true warrior. But Pandavas are in for more tragedies. My death won't give them peace."

The 17th day of war had ended.

Ashwatthama learnt that Bheema had smashed the thigh of Duryodhana and he was lying on the bank of a pond dying. He remembered the trick Pandavas had played to kill his father. This filled him with anger and he ran to Duryodhana and announced, "O Crown

Prince! You could not enjoy the throne. Neither will Pandavas. To night I shall murder Pandavas."

It pleased Duryodhana. He at once appointed him the Chief Commander of Kaurava army and said, "I was just waiting for you. I have faith in you that you will fulfil your promise and give peace to my soul."

The evening came and darkness spread around.

Ashwatthama could not go to sleep in his tent. He tried to think of a way to kill the Pandavas on the 18th day of the war, next day. But no worthwhile idea came to him. He came out of his tent and sat down under a tree to think.

He saw a strange act on the tree infront of him. An owl came and it killed many birds who were resting in their nests.

It showed Ashwatthama the way to dispose off the enemy. He planned to kill all the five Pandavas when they would be sleeping in their tents that night itself. He went into the tent of his uncle Kripacharya and revealed to him his plan.

Kripacharya rebuked him for his cowardly plan.

Ashwatthama screamed, "Uncle! How do you forget the cowardly manner in which they killed my father? Bheema hit Duryodhana on the thigh. Who cares for rules? Anyone helps me or not, I will put my plan in action."

Their voices brought Kritvarma also there who was in the next tent. On learning Ashwatthama's plan he also tried to dissuade him from going ahead. But Asthwatthama was adamant. When he prepared to go it alone, Kripacharya and Kritvarma too had to accompany him.

They slipped into the tent where Pandavas usually used to sleep. On that night they were not there. Krishna had taken them somewhere else. In their place, the five sons of Draupadi were sleeping. Ashwatthama beheaded them one by one. No one got wind of it.

Then, they stole into Dhrishtadhyumana's tent and beheaded him in sleep. Other Panchal warriors who were sleeping there also got killed.

All three did more killing in the nearby tents. It was a massacre of sleeping people. After killing they set fire to entire camp.

Then, the three came to the place where Duryodhana lay fatally wounded. Ashwatthama told him what they had done. When Duryodhana learnt that barring seven, all of the Pandava family had been slain he smiled. It gave great satisfaction to Duryodhana. He died with a smile on his face.

The next day, when Pandavas learnt about the massacre in their camp, they were grief stricken. It greatly angered them. Draupadi was devastated when she was given the news of the murder of her sons in cold blood. She wailed and cried. Pandavas tried to console her.

All five brothers picked up their arms and set out in search of the persons responsible for the dastardly act. It took little time for them to know that Ashwatthama had done it. They looked for him everywhere. At last they traced him out in the hut of sage Vyasa. He was hiding there.

The sight of Pandavas frightened him. To honour his vow he picked up a straw and threw it after sacred invocation, "Go! Destroy the seed of Pandavas if there is any in any womb."

The invoked straw became a sword and flew away to where Abhimanyu's widow Uttara sat. Luckily Krishna was present there. He knew what the sword was for. He at once de-activated it and protected foetus that was in Uttara's womb. This child later became famous as King Parikshit.

In the very vicinity of Vayasa's hut, a mace duel was fought by Bheema and Ashwatthama. Bheema defeated Ashwatthama. He had a divine gem embedded in his forehead which made him immortal. He surrendered it to Pandavas.

And with that incident, the 18 day war of Mahabharata came to an end.

❑ ❑

PANDAVAS IN HASTINAPUR PALACE

When Dhritrashtra learnt about the death of Duryodhana and the sons of Draupadi, he wailed in grief. He lamented, "By slaying Draupadi's sons Ashwatthama has destroyed the line of Hastinapur royal family." Sage Vidura consoled him.

Sage Vyasa also gave his sermon to the King, "Son! This war was essential. So, calm down. Accept Yudhishthira as your own son and live happily ever after. Let the past be dead."

Just then, Pandavas and Krishna arrived there. Dhritrashtra embraced them calling "Dear sons." It was just an play acting. What else could he do?

After taking leave of the King, Pandavas went to pay obeisance to Gandhari. She was grieving for her sons. Still she blessed Pandavas truthfully and blamed her brother and Duryodhana for the war.

Then, Pandavas proceeded to the bank of Ganga and performed the posthumous rites of all near and dear ones killed in the war.

Although, Yudhishthira was now unchallenged ruler of Hastinapur yet happiness eluded him. He was gloomy. One day, when he sat brooding, sage Narada arrived. The King revealed to him the reason for his sadness. He was most grieved at the death of Karna. He had come to know that Karna was the eldest son of mother Kunti. Narada told him the entire story of the birth of Karna. After learning the truth he spoke in anguish to Kunti, "Mother! You concealed the birth of brother Karna from all. That's what makes me so unhappy. So, I put a curse on woman kind that in future, no woman shall be able to keep her pregnancy a secret."

Infact, Yudhishthira had become so disenchanted that he wanted to renounce the throne and go into exile. All the four brothers and Draupadi tried to calm him down. They wanted him to prepare himself to get crowned. Sage Vyasa arrived there at that moment. He gave sermons to Yudhishthira and made him agree to become the King.

The coronation of Yudhishthira was celebreted with great fanfare. After becoming King, Yudhishthira went to Bhishma who waited sun to northernly. He gave the new King valuable advice and breathed his last. He was given a state funeral. The funeral again sent Yudhishthira in brooding mood. Bheema consoled him and Dhritrashtra gave him advice and consolation.

Krishna returned to Dwarika after Bhishma's funeral.

❏ ❏

DHRITRASHTRA-GANDHARI & KUNTI GO TO FORESTS

Now Hastinapur was under Pandava rule of King Yudhishthira. Under his rule the kingdom had become a welfare state. The people lived peacefully. He performed several Yajnas including Ashwamedha. Yudhishthira and his brothers looked after the three elders, Kunti, Dhritrashtra and Gandhari. Kunti took great care of Gandhari. So did Draupadi in respect of Kunti. And Gandhari adored them both.

Yudhishthira was honestly devoted to old Dhritrashtra. But Bheema often uttered taunts to him which hurt the old man very deeply. After a long time, Dhirtrashtra and Gandhari decided to renounce the royel life in favour of the life of forests.

One day, they said to Yudhishthira, "Son! You have been taking great care of us for the past fifteen years. We greatly appreciate it. Now we want to do penance in the rest days of our lives. You rule the Kingdom faithfully. We pray for your happiness and prosperity."

But Yudishthira was reluctant. Dhritrashtra asked priest Kripacharya and Vidura to plead with Yudhishthira to allow them to depart. Sage Vyasa also arrived there. They all put pressure on Yudhishthira to accept the old couple's wish.

When Dhritrashtra and Gandhari made preparations to go, Kunti too became restless. She also wanted to go with them. Yudhishthira had to agree. All the three old people proceeded to forests. Before departure, Kinti said to her King son, "Son! Don't ever forget your brother Karna. And take due care of my Nakula and Sahdeva. That's my order to you."

The three lived in forests for three years. Then, one day the forest caught fire and all of them perished.

❑ ❑

LORD KRISHNA DEPARTS

Krishna ruled over Dwarika for 36 years.

One day, a group of sages arrived at Dwarika. A prince named Samba, put on the guise of a pregnant woman as a prank and went to the sages and asked, "O great sages! Tell me, will it be a son or a daughter?"

The eldest of the sages saw through the trick and prophesied, "A pastle will be born to you that will destroy your dynasty."

Due to the curse, Yadavas of Dwarika fell out with one another and fought among themselves with pastles and their self-destruction began. Balrama grieved over the situation and died. Krishna went to forests and rested under a tree. He fell asleep. A hunter saw the feet of sleeping Krishna and mistook it for a part of a deer. He shot his arrow. It found its aim. And Krishna departed for his heavenly abode.

When the news of the downfall of Yadavas and the demise of Krishna reached Hastinapur, Pandavas too decided to depart on pilgrimage as prelude to the final journey to the after world. They handed over the reigns to Abhimanyu's son Parikshit and set out. After visiting several pilgrim centres Pandavas and Draupadi reached the foot hills of Himalayas. A dog joined the party and travelled with them. After crossing several valleys and mountain passes, they reached Himadri hill. Beyond was snow and snow. The party walked on braving the cold and the slipperiness of the snow. Yudhishthira travelled without trouble. Others faced problems. Draupadi was the first to slip down into a snow gorge and die. Then, one by one, Arjuna, Nakula, Sahdeva and Bheema died. Yudhishthira kept going regardless followed by the dog. Their journey continued through glaciers and snow valleys.

The dog was infact Dharamraja who wanted to test the righteousness of Yudhishthira.

Suddenly, Yudhishthira sighted a heavenly chariot in which sat Lord Indra. The chariot stopped near him. He paid obeisance to Indra. After blessing Indra said, "Yudhishthira! Your brothers and Draupadi has reached the distination. You are the symbol of Dharma. So, I came to take you to heavens alive. Come, ride on my chariot."

Yudhishthira agreed and began mounting the chariot. The dog also tried to get on after him. Indira shooed away the dog saying that there was no place for a dog in heaven.

Yudhishthira said, "Lord! This dog is with me all through the hill and snow journeys. He stuck to me. Hence, I will also stick to him. If there is no place for my dog in heaven, then I won't like to go to such heaven." He got down. Indra's pleading made no impression on him. He stood his ground.

Then, the dog transformed into Dharamraja. He blessed

Yudhishthira for his loyalty and compassion before disappearing.

After that Yudhishthira reached the heaven in the chariot. There he found Duryodhana sitting on a high throne. But to his shock he saw Draupadi and his brothers rotting and burning in hell. He thundered, "O Angels! Tell me, what wrong my brothers and Draupadi has done to deserve this? What great deed Kauravas have done to be rewarded a place in heaven?"

He cursed the justice of God. He spoke to the angel who had escorted him to the hell, "Go back! I don't want to come with you to the heaven. I will stay here. How can I live in heaven when my dear brothers and faithful Draupadi is burning in hell?"

The angel returned to the heaven. Yudhishthira stood dumbfounded. He was very sad and pained. How could all that happen, he could not understand. A long time passed. He stayed burning in hell. Then, Indra and Dharamaraja appeared there and hell scene disappeared. The sounds of crying and wailing stopped. There was no more rotten smell of hell. Dharamaraja spoke, "We tested you on every step. You passed all tests. You rejected heaven for the sake of your wife and brothers. So we come here. O ture One! Do you want any explanation?"

"Yes, Father! Why all those tests for me? What was the objective behind it?"

"Son! You have been an ideal King. The true Kings must experience the heat of the hell to stay truthful. That's why we gave you a taste of hell." Then he added, "Don't grieve. All your near and dear ones are in the heaven. No one is in hell. All that hell scene was illusion for your test. You are in heaven right here. Look, there is sage Narada."

This revelation greatly pleased Yudhishthira. Then, he freed his soul from the human body. He found his elder brother Karna, younger brothers, Draupadi, Kauravas and others duly enjoying the peace of the heaven. And his soul settled down in heaven's eternal peace.

❏ ❏

SAGE VYASA'S MESSAGE

After creating the epic 'Mahabharata', Sage Vyasa had it read out by his son, Shukdeva and summed it up. "Truth is religion. Nothing in this would is above religion. It gives salvation, meaning and purpose to life. Don't trade religion for desires, greed, survival or physical security. The religion is for ever. Happiness and sadness are passing phases. The soul is immortal. The body is temporary."

The soul message of Mahabharata is as fruitful as the study of the entire epic. Making it the guiding principle of everyday life will lead to *Nirvana*.

□ □ □